Loveland, Colorado

HolyWord Studios Director Manual

Visit our Web site: **www.grouppublishing.com**

Credits
HolyWord Studios Coordinator: Jody Brolsma
Chief Creative Officer: Joani Schultz
Copy Editors: Pamela Shoup and Janis Sampson
Art Director: Kari K. Monson
Cover Art Director: Lisa Chandler
Cover Photographer: L.D. Bohm, Bohm/Marrazzo Photography
Cover Designer: Andrea Boven
Illustrator: Bryan Bandyk
Production Manager: Peggy Naylor

ISBN 0-7644-2173-5
Printed in the United States of America.
10 9 8 7 6 5 4 3 2 1   01 00

Contents

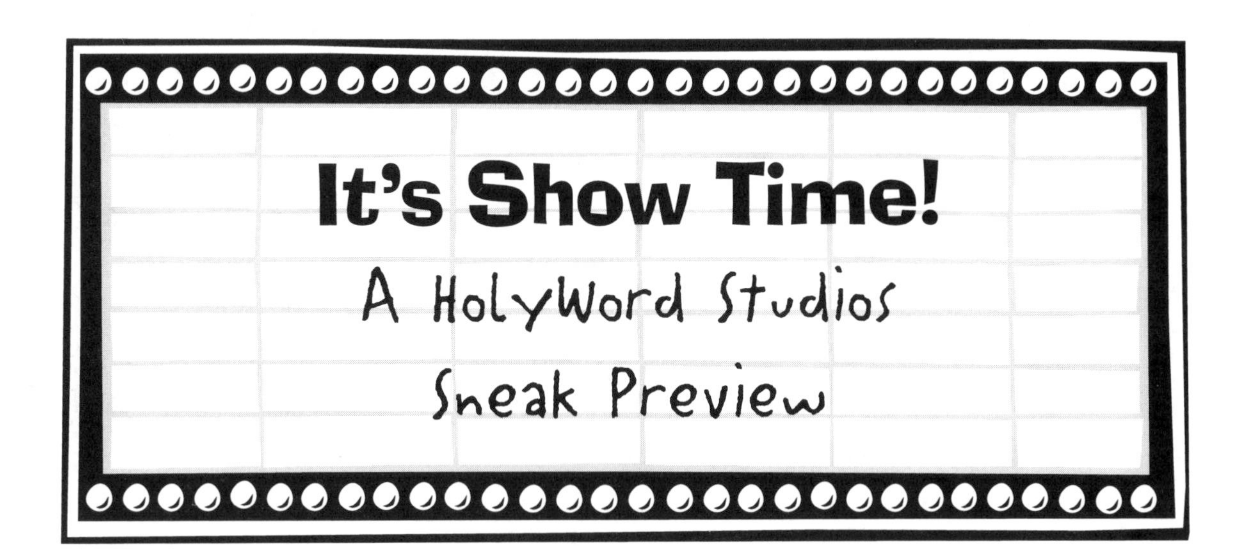
It's Show Time!
A HolyWord Studios
Sneak Preview

Welcome to HolyWord Studios!

Lights, camera...action! The camera is rolling, the cast is ready, and production is about to begin! So get ready to be part of a blockbuster event that gets two thumbs up from kids, teenagers, and adults everywhere. HolyWord Studios is proud to bring you a VBS program where kids star in God's story.

If you haven't used Group's VBS materials before, you're in for a real treat. HolyWord Studios is an exciting, fun-filled, Bible-based program your kids will love. (We know because we tested everything in a field test last summer. Look for tips entitled "A Cue From Our Crew" to learn what we discovered and how that will make *your* program the best!) Your teachers will love being cast and crew members at HolyWord Studios, too, because their roles are so easy! And *you'll* love it because kids will star in God's story, using the Bible as their script.

Each day at HolyWord Studios is packed with activities designed to help kids understand their role in God's story. Kids start off each day by forming small groups called Film Crews. All the Film Crews gather at Sing & Play Soundtrack to do fun motions to upbeat Bible songs. Then Film Crews "scout" five different Locations. They meet Chadder Chipmunk™ on video, get into the "action" at Now Playing Games, sample tasty Movie Munchies, explore the excitement and drama of Blockbuster Bible Adventures, and visit Prop Shop Crafts to make creations that get two thumbs up from *every* cast member. Then crews gather together to participate in each day's Show Time. And throughout the week, children work on a special production they'll share during Operation Kid-to-Kid™. This missions project allows the kids at your church to impact children around the globe!

Preschoolers have a special HolyWord Studios program of their own in the Preschool Bible Playhouse. The Preschool Bible Playhouse Director Manual contains complete instructions for setting up, organizing, and running the Preschool Bible Playhouse.

This HolyWord Studios Director Manual contains everything you need to plan a successful program, recruit and train volunteers, publicize your program, and follow up with kids and their families after your HolyWord Studios production "wraps." **The cameras are rolling! So get ready to put your kids front and center in God's amazing story!**

HolyWord HiNtS

Make this Director Manual even easier to use! Cut away the binding, then use a three-hole punch to make holes near the spine. Place the pages in a three-ring binder, with divider pages separating each section.

HolyWord HiNtS

As Studio Director, you'll want to know what's happening each day. Refer to the "HolyWord Studios Overview Chart" on pages 10-11 to get an overview of the Bible stories and biblical truths elementary kids cover. You'll discover how these truths are reinforced creatively throughout each day. Also, look for the camera icon next to certain activities. This icon lets you know which activities will look great on video, in case you decide to make your own "movie." For more info on videotaping your VBS, check out the "Creating a 'Reel' HolyWord Studios Production" section on page 162.

HolyWord Studios Overview

This is what everyone else is doing! At HolyWord Studios, the daily Bible Point is carefully integrated into each Location activity to reinforce Bible learning. Each Location is an important part of kids' overall learning experience.

	BIBLE POINT	BIBLE STORY	BIBLE VERSE	SING & PLAY SOUNDTRACK	PROP SHOP CRAFTS	NOW PLAYING GAMES
DAY 1	**God cares for us.**	Baby Moses is saved from death (Exodus 1:1–2:10).	"For your Father knows what you need before you ask him" (Matthew 6:8b).	• I Walk by Faith • Ha-Le-La-Le-La-Le-Lu-Jah • God's Story (Chorus and Day 1 only)	**Craft** TLSeed Necklace **Application** Just as God watched over Moses and cared for him, kids will care for their bean seeds and watch them grow.	**Games** • River Run • In a Holy Pickle • Bombs Away • Bound to Get Soaked • River Basket Relay **Application** God cares for us, and we can rest in his care.
DAY 2	**God protects us.**	God protects the Israelites from the plagues (Exodus 7:1–10:29).	"Come to me, all you who are weary and burdened, and I will give you rest" (Matthew 11:28).	• God Is Good All the Time • Shout to the Lord • Trust in the Lord With All Your Heart • God's Story (Chorus and Days 1 and 2)	**Craft** Yahoo Yo-Yos **Application** With this timeless toy, kids will remember the "ups and downs" that the Israelites faced during the plagues. They'll also be reminded that God never let go of his people.	**Games** • What's That? • Under Attack • Like the Plague • Storyboards • Plague Trap **Application** God protects us, and we can look to him for help.
DAY 3	**God loves us.**	God spares the Israelites during Passover and allows them to cross the Red Sea (Exodus 11:1–15:21).	"In the same way your Father in heaven is not willing that any of these little ones should be lost" (Matthew 18:14).	• Look What God Is Doing • If the Lord Had Not Been on Our Side • Joy • God's Story (Chorus, Days 1, 2, and 3)	**Craft** The Incredi-Ball **Application** These colorful, bouncing balls will amaze and delight kids while reminding them of God's miraculous power and love for us.	**Games** • Red Sea Rally • Leader of the Crowd • Tiny Bubbles • Sea Blast • Gone Fishin' **Application** God loves us just as much as he loved the Israelites.
DAY 4	**God saves us.**	Jesus is crucified and rises from the dead (Matthew 27:11–28:7).	"She will give birth to a son, and you are to give him the name Jesus, because he will save his people from their sins" (Matthew 1:21).	• We Believe in God • Jesus Loves Me Rock • God's Story (Chorus, Days 1, 2, 3, and 4)	**Craft** Amazing Pictures **Application** This amazing craft reminds kids that, while life without Jesus is like an old black-and-white movie, our lives are transformed and brightened when we have a relationship with Jesus.	**Games** • Jesus Saves Relay • Socks on Your Head • Yuck! • Set Me Free • Goop Relay **Application** Our lives can be changed because Jesus rose from the dead.
DAY 5	**God is always with us.**	The Holy Spirit comes at Pentecost (Acts 2:1-47).	"Therefore go and make disciples of all nations, baptizing them in the name of the Father and of the Son and of the Holy Spirit...And surely I am with you always, to the very end of the age" (Matthew 28:19-20).	• Praise Him • Go!! • God's Story (Entire song)	**Craft** Operation Kid-to-Kid Care Kits **Application** As kids create their Care Kits, they'll discover that they can share God's love with children around the world.	**Games** • Make a Mark • Freeze Frame Stomp • All-Star Olympics • The Name Game • Outreach Tag **Application** Since God is always with us, we can have confidence to stand up for him.

This overview chart shows you the entire program at a glance. Refer to the chart to see how each Location's activities supplement other activities to help kids star in God's story.

MOVIE MUNCHIES	CHADDER'S ADVENTURE THEATER	BLOCKBUSTER BIBLE ADVENTURES	SHOW TIME
Snack Moses in a Basket **Application** God cared for Moses when Moses was a baby. Today's snack shows that God cares for people—even tiny babies.	**Video Segment** While excitedly telling about his starring role in a movie, Chadder accidentally activates a "fake" time machine and is transported back to Egypt thousands of years ago. There he meets a new friend, Carmine Camel, who has discovered baby Moses in a basket in the river. The adventurers watch as Pharaoh's daughter finds the baby. Then they run back to the time machine to attempt an escape before Pharaoh's guards see them! **Application** • How do we know God cares for us? • How does God show that he cares for us each day? • Mark your Student Book at Matthew 6:8b.	 • Star in the Bible story by placing a paper "baby" in a basket in "the Nile." • Experience what it might have been like to stand up to an Egyptian soldier. • Discuss how God cared for baby Moses.	• Use balloons to demonstrate how God wants us to let go of our worries. • Use cotton candy to discover how worries can "melt away." • Receive mini hand clappers as reminders that we are always in God's hands.
 **Snack** Bugs and Blood **Application** God protected the Israelites from the plagues that devastated the Egyptians. Today's snack reminds kids that God protected his people.	**Video Segment** Chadder and Carmine get to the time machine and take off without being caught. They land in Egypt just before the first Passover, where they are rescued by Hoppy, a frightened frog. Hoppy tells them how Pharaoh and the Egyptians have been cruel to God's people, the Israelites. Hoppy also tells about all the plagues and how God protected the Israelites when these bad things happened to the Egyptians. **Application** • How does God protect us? • Mark your Student Book at Matthew 11:28. • How can Matthew 11:28 remind us of what God does for us?	• Give Pharaoh nine chances to release the Israelites. • "Inflict" each of the first nine plagues on "Pharaoh." • Discuss how God cared for the Israelites.	• Watch water turn red to see what it might have been like when the water in the Nile turned to blood. • See how God's protection is like an umbrella, keeping us from a "storm" of harmful things. • Receive sunglasses to remind them that just as sunglasses protect our eyes from the sun, God protects us.
Snack Red Sea Splits **Application** God's miraculous parting of the Red Sea was motivated by the love he had for his people. Today's snack shows how God showed love for his people by delivering them from their Egyptian pursuers.	**Video Segment** After escaping from the palace, Chadder and his friends talk with two Israelite children who are preparing to leave Egypt after the Passover. They explain what happened, and Chadder learns how much God loves us. The adventurers escape into their time machine, just as the waters of the Red Sea start closing in. **Application** • How does it feel to know that God loves you? • Mark your Student Book at Matthew 18:14. • How does Matthew 18:14 show us how much God loves us?	 • Design sets by painting red paint on door posts. • Pray for family members, and experience a Passover meal. • Wait in silence as the angel of death passes over. • Tell a frightened scout that God will part the Red Sea.	 • Create the waving, wild Red Sea, using blue and green balloons. • Watch how the Israelites crossed the Red Sea on dry land. • Receive autograph pens as reminders that God loves us so much that he writes his name on our hearts.
 **Snack** Sweet Butterflies **Application** When Jesus rose from the dead, he established the means by which we receive new life. Each sweet treat is a perfect reminder of that new life.	 **Video Segment** The time machine whisks Chadder, Carmine, and Hoppy to Jerusalem, where Jesus has been crucified. Chadder remembers that the Bible says that Jesus rose from the dead. He explains that Jesus saves us through his death and resurrection. **Application** • How do you get to heaven? • What ways do people think they can get to heaven that don't work? • Mark your Student Book at Matthew 1:21. • What does Matthew 1:21 tell us about what Jesus did for us?	• Put their "sins" on a cross. • Create sound effects for a shadow presentation of the Crucifixion. • Experience the sadness of Jesus' death, and learn that he was our Passover lamb.	 • Use dissolving plastic to represent sins that are given to Jesus. • Watch as Jesus makes sins disappear. • Receive a mirror as a reminder of who Jesus saved.
 **Snack** Mini Birthday Cakes **Application** When God gave the Holy Spirit to Jesus' followers on the day of Pentecost, the church was born. Today's snack celebrates the birthday of the church.	 **Video Segment** Chadder and his friends jump into the time machine to escape a Roman guard. When the time machine stops again, they meet up with Mary who tells them about Jesus' resurrection and about the Holy Spirit coming upon Jesus' followers at Pentecost. We discover that all of Chadder's time travel has been a dream. He tells his friends at the movie studio about all of his adventures, and he comes away having learned that God is always with us. **Application** • What does the Holy Spirit do for us? • Mark your Student Book at Matthew 28:19-20. • How does the message of Matthew 28:19-20 help us?	 • Experience the confusion of trying to communicate using different languages. • Experience what it means to bring others into God's family. • Draw pictures of times they're glad God is with them. • Sing a song to celebrate God's presence in their lives.	 • Use gift boxes to represent each day's Point. • Present their Operation Kid-to-Kid packages as a special offering. • Receive bubbles as a reminder of the Holy Spirit and Pentecost.

Inspecting Your HolyWord Studios Starter Kit

Before you begin your HolyWord Studios program, inspect your Starter Kit to make sure it contains all the following items:

☆ **HolyWord Studios Director Manual (you're reading it now!)**—This is your guide to directing your HolyWord Studios production. It includes everything you need to plan, staff, and promote your church's best program ever! In it you'll find photocopiable handouts, letters, certificates, and more.

☆ ***Sneak Preview* video**—This video provides an overview of the entire HolyWord Studios program. As you watch the video, you'll meet teachers and kids who've participated in real HolyWord Studios productions. You'll see for yourself how much fun Bible learning can be. The video also contains training material so you can feel confident that your cast is well-prepared for its role in HolyWord Studios. Additionally, your HolyWord Studios Director Manual tells you how to use this video as a quick promotional tool to get your church, kids, parents, and teachers excited about your blockbuster program.

☆ **Preschool Bible Playhouse Director Manual**—This manual outlines five days of complete programs for children between the ages of three and five. The manual also contains supply lists, room setup and decoration ideas, exciting Bible-teaching ideas, and more to make your Preschool Bible Playhouse *the* place to be!

☆ **seven Location leader manuals:**

- **Sing & Play Soundtrack Leader Manual**
- **Movie Munchies Leader Manual**
- **Prop Shop Crafts Leader Manual**
- **Blockbuster Bible Adventures Leader Manual**
- **Chadder's Adventure Theater Leader Manual***
- **Now Playing Games Leader Manual**
- **Show Time Leader Manual**

Each leader manual introduction contains detailed instructions for before, during, and after HolyWord Studios, plus an overview of the entire program. Leader manuals include clear, step-by-step directions for each activity, guided discussion questions, valuable "HolyWord Hints," and "A Cue From Our Crew" to make sure everything goes smoothly.

*Requires *Chadder's HolyWord Adventure* video (available from Group Publishing, Inc. and your local Christian bookstore).

HolyWord HiNtS

Before you hand the leader manuals to your Location Leaders, be sure to skim the books to get an idea of what's happening in each area. You'll feel better prepared to answer questions that may arise.

☆ ***Sing & Play Soundtrack* audiocassette**—This audiocassette provides Bible songs your kids will love, including the HolyWord Studios theme song, "God's Story." The cassette is recorded in split-track format so you can use just the accompaniment or can add kids' voices. After you've listened to the cassette, give it to your Sing & Play Soundtrack Leader. He or she will use the cassette to teach kids the HolyWord Studios songs. You may want to order additional cassettes so other leaders (especially those for Prop Shop Crafts, Movie Munchies, and Now Playing Games) can play the songs in the background as kids visit their Locations.

☆ **Operation Kid-to-Kid brochure**—On Day 2, kids will learn about an exciting, meaningful missions project called Operation Kid-to-Kid. In Operation Kid-to-Kid, the children at your VBS will send Care Kits to needy children around the world. This brochure explains what Operation Kid-to-Kid is, how it was developed, who it will impact, and how the kids at your VBS will carry it out.

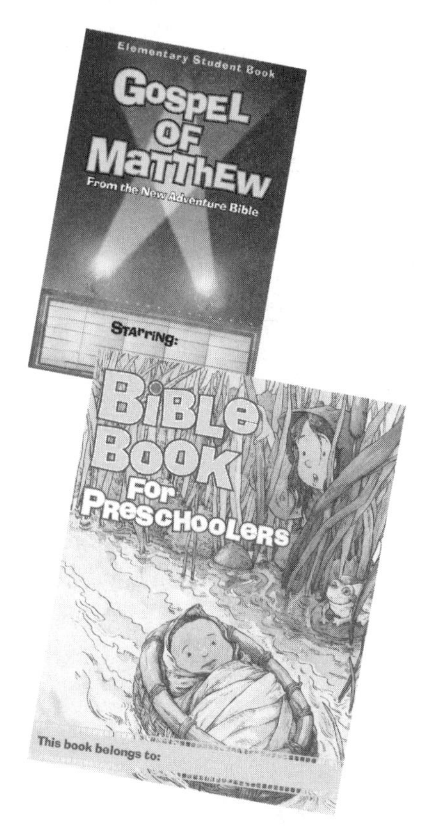

☆ **Elementary Student Book**—There's no better book for kids to explore than God's Word! That's why kids at HolyWord Studios will use the New International Version of the Gospel of Matthew as their Student Books. During HolyWord Studios, children will read, highlight, and create helpful tabs in their Bible books. The kids at your VBS will discover that the Bible is like a script, giving us direction in life. Plus, each Student Book includes items to get kids started on their Care Kits for Operation Kid-to-Kid.

☆ **Preschool Student Book**—Preschoolers get to discover God's amazing story in their own age-appropriate children's Bible books. Children will add stickers to the Bible book pages to help them remember the significance of each story. Preschool Student Books also include exciting activity pages for children to work on, plus ideas for family activities that will reinforce the Point at home. And, the Preschool Student Book contains Care Kit items so children of all ages can participate in Operation Kid-to-Kid.

☆ **craft packet**—Use the items in this packet to create samples of all the cool Prop Shop Crafts. Kids will love these irresistible, engaging crafts, like TLSeed Necklaces, Yahoo Yo-Yos, Incredi-Balls, and Amazing Pictures. (Inside the packet, you'll find an informative flier that lists the enclosed items and shows what the finished crafts look like.)

☆ **Operation Kid-to-Kid bags**—You'll use these twenty-five bags to hold Care Kits—health and hygiene items for needy children around the world. Not only will the recipients use the Care Kit items, they'll use these resealable bags to carry fresh water! (Twenty-five bags is sufficient for a VBS of up to 125 children. If you need more bags, contact Group Publishing or your local Christian bookstore.)

☆ **Magnificent Megaphone**—This is just one of the crafts preschoolers will make at HolyWord Studios. They'll decorate the Magnificent Megaphones with bright stickers, then use the megaphones to shout out the good news of God's love. (For information about other preschool crafts, check out the craft packet, also in your Starter Kit.)

☆ **bag of sample items**—Add dazzle to your production with these "extras." In this bag you'll find publicity aids to help you build excitement about your program, awards to recognize everyone's contribution, and souvenirs to leave a lasting impression.

If any Starter Kit items are missing or damaged, contact your local Christian bookstore for prompt replacement.

If you checked off everything on this list, you're ready to start production at HolyWord Studios!

May God bless you as you plan your HolyWord Studios program!

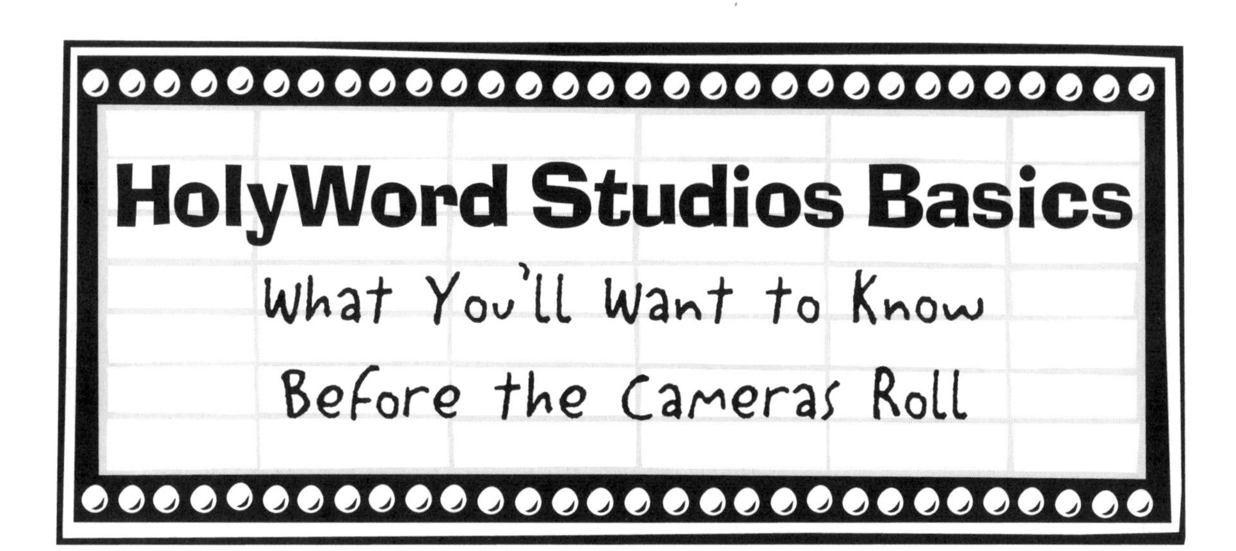

HolyWord Studios Basics

What You'll Want to Know Before the Cameras Roll

Why HolyWord Studios?

What makes Group's HolyWord Studios different from other VBS programs?

• **At HolyWord Studios, kids learn one important Bible Point each day.** Instead of trying to teach kids more than they can remember or apply, HolyWord Studios focuses on one key biblical concept. The Bible Point is reinforced daily through Bible stories, Bible verses, songs, and hands-on activities that help kids discover that the Bible is like a script, directing us through life and showing that God has a plan for everyone. Kids who attend your church regularly will enjoy discovering this important truth in fresh, new ways. And neighborhood kids who come to your VBS will hear the "meat" of the gospel right away. Each day kids will learn something new about God.

Day 1: God cares for us.
Day 2: God protects us.
Day 3: God loves us.
Day 4: God saves us.
Day 5: God is always with us.

• **At HolyWord Studios, kids learn the way they learn best.** Not all kids learn the same way, so HolyWord Studios offers seven daily Locations to meet the needs of all kinds of learners. Each child will come away from each day remembering the Bible Point because kids will pick it up in a way that matches their learning style.

Sing & Play Soundtrack's songs and motions will teach the Bible Point to your **musical learners.**

Now Playing Games, Blockbuster Bible Adventures, and Prop Shop Crafts allow **bodily-kinesthetic learners** to wiggle and move as they explore the Bible Point in active ways.

Chadder's Adventure Theater lets **visual learners** discover the Bible Point through watching the *Chadder's HolyWord Adventure* video.

Movie Munchies allows **interpersonal learners** the opportunity to explore God's story as they make and serve snacks for the entire cast and crew at HolyWord Studios.

Don't overlook the impact this program can have on teens and adults. Learners of all ages benefit from the active, fresh Bible story presentations at HolyWord Studios. We've heard from youth and adults who said their hearts were touched, lives were changed, and faith was renewed after experiencing these Bible truths in such new ways!

Show Time's dramatic and interactive programs help **linguistic learners** remember each day's Bible Point.

Every Location asks meaningful, thought-provoking questions that encourage **logical and introspective learners** to think about and apply the Bible Point.

• **At HolyWord Studios, teachers teach the way they teach best.** Just like kids, not all teachers think alike. Instead of forcing every teacher to teach the same material, HolyWord Studios provides opportunities for you to cast a variety of teachers in the roles that best suit them. Got a great storyteller in your congregation? Cast that person in leading Blockbuster Bible Adventures. Got a great athlete? Cast that person in the "lead role" at Now Playing Games. Because each Location is different, teachers can volunteer in their areas of expertise. And volunteers who are intimidated by the idea of teaching can join your cast and crew as Film Crew Leaders.

HolyWord HINTS

We've heard it again and again from VBS Directors everywhere: "This program brought out people's talents in wonderful new ways! People who never imagined that they could work with kids had a great time—and already volunteered to help next year!" So go for it! Look beyond "the usual" group of volunteers and bring in some new faces.

• **At HolyWord Studios, no activity stands alone.** Instead of leading independent, isolated classes, Location Leaders see all the kids each day. Sing & Play Soundtrack songs play in the background during other activities. One of the crafts kids make during Prop Shop Crafts is given as an offering during Show Time. The Now Playing Games Leader serves as an assistant Movie Munchies chef. All Location Leaders assist in Show Time. Each member of your HolyWord Studios cast and crew provides a unique and important part of kids' total VBS experience. With everyone working together, your staff will breeze through the week.

• **At HolyWord Studios, kids take responsibility for what they're learning.** Throughout the week, kids travel to Locations with their Film Crews—small groups of three to five kids. On the first day, each child chooses a job that he or she will do throughout the week. Kids may be Readers, Studio Guides, Materials Managers, Cheerleaders, or Prayer People. From time to time, Location Leaders will call on kids to complete tasks that are part of their job descriptions.

Each Film Crew also has an adult or teenage Film Crew Leader. Film Crew Leaders aren't teachers. They're simply part of Film Crew families—like older brothers or sisters. Film Crew Leaders participate in all the activities and encourage kids to talk about and apply what they're learning. Film Crew Leaders who participated in HolyWord Studios field tests saw kids encouraging other kids during the activities, helping younger crew members with difficult tasks, and reminding each other to use kind words. At HolyWord Studios, kids put God's Word into action!

• **At HolyWord Studios, everyone is treated with respect.** Because kids travel in combined-age Film Crews, big kids and little kids learn to work together. Instead of trying to compete with children their own age, older children help younger children during Prop Shop Crafts and Now Playing Games. Younger children spark older children's imaginations during Blockbuster Bible Adventures and Show Time.

Studies show that children learn as much—or more—when they're linked with kids of different ages. In fact, one study observed that children naturally chose to play with other children their age only 6 percent of the time. They played with children at least one year older or younger than them 55 percent of the time.

Think of Film Crews as families in which kids naturally learn with and from one another. Social skills improve, self-esteem rises, cooperation increases, and discipline problems diminish.

A Cue From Our Crew

"The older kids at my church like being with their friends. They'll complain if they have to be with the 'little' kids." Many people are hesitant to try teaching combined-age groups because they're afraid kids will balk at something new. You can let kids partner with same-age friends if they're really reluctant. But at our field tests, we discovered that kids enjoyed being in combined-age Film Crews. Sure, it was a little different at first, but as kids warmed up to their crew mates, we saw them working together, helping each other, and forming friendships. There were few complaints, and discipline problems were almost nonexistent.

Combined-age Film Crews also allow people of any age (even entire families) to join you for your HolyWord Studios program. You can even use combined-age Film Crews to teach kids about being part of the body of Christ!

Knowing and understanding these distinctions will help you present HolyWord Studios to your church or committee.

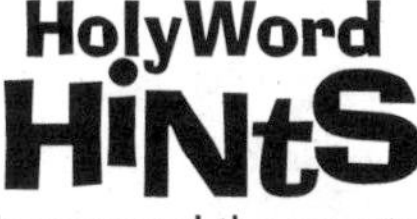

Churches around the country have reported great success with having families travel together as crews! Family crews build unity, encourage communication, and create wonderful memories that families will cherish for years to come.

How Will Kids Learn the Bible?

Each day, kids will be exposed to a Bible Point as well as to a corresponding Bible story and verse. The chart on page 20 shows the Bible content kids will cover each day.

A Cue From Our Crew

You'll notice that all of the memory verses are from the Gospel of Matthew. Since children use the book of Matthew as their Student Book, we selected passages that kids could look up, highlight, and tab during VBS. These Bibles become long-term helps—not merely throwaway student books. In fact, we've seen kids a year after VBS still reading from their special VBS Bibles! What a super way to make Bible memory meaningful, easy, and fun!

Day	Bible Point	Bible Story	Bible Verse
1	God cares for us.	Baby Moses is saved from death (Exodus 1:1–2:10).	"For your Father knows what you need before you ask him" (Matthew 6:8b).
2	God protects us.	God protects the Israelites from the plagues (Exodus 7:1–10:29).	"Come to me, all you who are weary and burdened, and I will give you rest" (Matthew 11:28).
3	God loves us.	God spares the Israelites during Passover and allows them to cross the Red Sea (Exodus11:1–15:21).	"In the same way your Father in heaven is not willing that any of these little ones should be lost" (Matthew 18:14).
4	God saves us.	Jesus is crucified and rises from the dead (Matthew 27:11–28:7).	"She will give birth to a son, and you are to give him the name Jesus, because he will save his people from their sins" (Matthew 1:21).
5	God is always with us.	The Holy Spirit comes at Pentecost (Acts 2:1-47).	"Therefore go and make disciples of all nations, baptizing them in the name of the Father and of the Son and of the Holy Spirit...And surely I am with you always, to the very end of the age" (Matthew 28:19-20).

HolyWord HINTS

At each Location, kids will be carefully listening to hear the Bible Point so they can respond by clapping and shouting, "Action!" Watch their excitement and enthusiasm—and listening skills—build throughout the week!

HolyWord HINTS

You'll need to be available during Sing & Play Soundtrack. The Sing & Play Leader will send all the Film Crew Leaders out of the room for a brief time of prayer with you. Then you'll come forward at the end of Sing & Play to give announcements, pray, and send Film Crews to their first Locations.

If you usually incorporate memory verses into your program, you can have kids memorize the daily Bible verses provided in this chart. Since children actually look up and read the key verses during Chadder's Adventure Theater, it's a natural connection!

At each Location, kids will encounter a different presentation of the Bible Point, Bible story, or Bible verse.

Sing & Play Soundtrack

- The Sing & Play Soundtrack Leader repeats the Bible Point each day.
- In addition to fun praise songs, kids sing at least one song each day that specifically ties to that day's Bible Point.
- Each day kids learn a new verse of the HolyWord Studios theme song, "God's Story." Each day's verse focuses on the corresponding daily Bible story.
- Each day the Sing & Play Soundtrack Leader summarizes the daily Bible story.

Prop Shop Crafts

- The Prop Shop Crafts Leader repeats the Bible Point each day.
- Kids make crafts that remind them of each day's Bible story. For example, on Day 1 children make TLSeed Necklaces (that contain seeds which actually grow!) to remind them of how God cared for and watched over Moses, when Moses was a baby.
- Kids listen to the Sing & Play Soundtrack songs as they're working.

• The Prop Shop Crafts Leader asks questions to help kids review and apply the Bible Point and the Bible story.

• Kids experience what it means to share God's love through Operation Kid-to-Kid.

Chadder's Adventure Theater

• In each day's video segment, Chadder Chipmunk hears the daily Bible Point and the Bible story.

• The Chadder's Adventure Theater Leader repeats the Bible Point each day.

• Kids apply Chadder's experiences to their own lives through role-play, problem-solving, and other short activities.

• Kids look up, read, and tab key Bible verses to see how the Bible directs us in life.

Movie Munchies

• The Movie Munchies Leader repeats the Bible Point each day.

• Kids make and eat snacks that reinforce the daily Bible story, such as Moses in a Basket (Day 1) and Mini Birthday Cakes (Day 5).

• Kids show God's love by serving others. Each day one set of Film Crews makes the snacks for the entire VBS—even the preschoolers!

• Kids listen to Sing & Play Soundtrack songs as they make and eat their snacks.

Now Playing Games

• The Now Playing Games Leader repeats the Bible Point each day.

• Kids play games that encourage them to apply what they've learned. For example, on Day 1 kids apply the Bible Point, "God cares for us" by trying to gently pass water balloons with partners.

• Kids listen to Sing & Play Soundtrack songs as they play games.

• The Now Playing Games Leader connects each game to the daily Bible Point.

Blockbuster Bible Adventures

• The Blockbuster Bible Adventures Leader repeats the Bible Point each day.

• Kids experience the daily Bible story in a hands-on way. For example, on Day 3, kids experience the anticipation and anxiety of Passover, as they paint "door frames" red and pray for God to protect those who they love.

Show Time

• The Show Time Leader repeats the Bible Point each day.

• Kids repeat the Sing & Play Soundtrack songs they've learned that day.

• Kids use drama to apply what they've learned throughout the day. For example, on Day 3 they use a "sea" of balloons to act out the story of the parting of the Red Sea.

Preschool Bible Playhouse

• Preschoolers sing the Sing & Play Soundtrack songs with the older kids.

• The Preschool Bible Playhouse Director tells each day's Bible story in a fun, involving way.

Chadder's Adventure Theater is more than just time to watch a video—this is where kids really dig into Bible reading and life-application. In our field tests, we've discovered that the mix of video and Bible exploration is an excellent tool for reaching a variety of learners. Kids have the opportunity to work with an actual Bible, as well as make the life-application connections that cement Bible learning.

• The Preschool Bible Playhouse Director repeats the Bible Point during each Location Station activity.

• Preschoolers hear the Bible story and the Bible Point as they watch *Chadder's HolyWord Adventure.*

• Preschoolers make and eat snacks that reinforce the daily Bible story.

• Preschoolers sing additional songs that reinforce the daily Bible Point or Bible story.

• Preschoolers participate in Show Time with the older kids.

As you can see, HolyWord Studios is packed with Bible-based activities your kids will love!

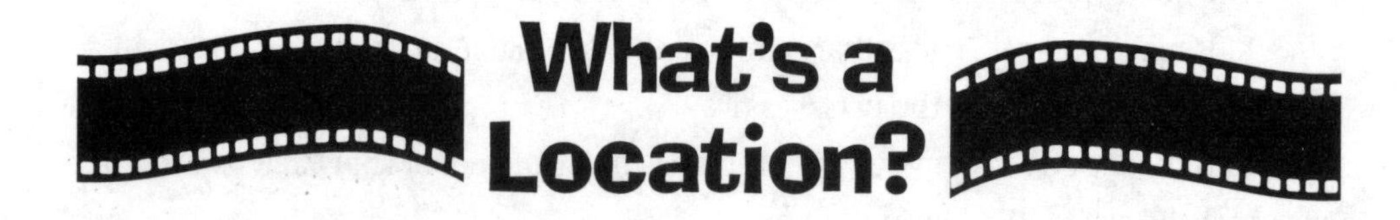

What's a Location?

HolyWord HiNtS

On Day 1 only, preschoolers skip Sing & Play Soundtrack and go straight to Preschool Bible Playhouse. This allows little ones to meet their Preschool Director, Film Crew Leaders, and Film Crew members. Plus preschoolers get to make Movie Munchies on Day 1, and the extra time helps them accomplish this *big* task!

HolyWord HiNtS

Middle schoolers and high schoolers make excellent Assistant Location Leaders. Not only do these older kids enjoy leadership roles, but they also provide super role models for children!

At HolyWord Studios, kids dig into Bible learning as they visit various Locations each day. Each Location features a different Bible-learning activity. Some Locations—such as Sing & Play Soundtrack, Movie Munchies, and Show Time—accommodate all the HolyWord Studios "cast" simultaneously. Kids will visit other Locations in smaller groups.

Elementary-age kids visit the following Locations each day:

- Sing & Play Soundtrack
- Prop Shop Crafts
- Now Playing Games
- Movie Munchies
- Chadder's Adventure Theater
- Blockbuster Bible Adventures
- Show Time

Preschoolers spend most of their time in the Preschool Bible Playhouse, but they visit the following Locations each day:

- Sing & Play Soundtrack
- Chadder's Adventure Theater
- Show Time

Each Location is staffed by an adult leader. If you have more than 150 kids in your program, you may want to assign two adult leaders to each Location. They can team teach a large group of kids or can set up identical Locations for two smaller groups in separate areas.

If you have up to 150 kids, your church might be set up like this...

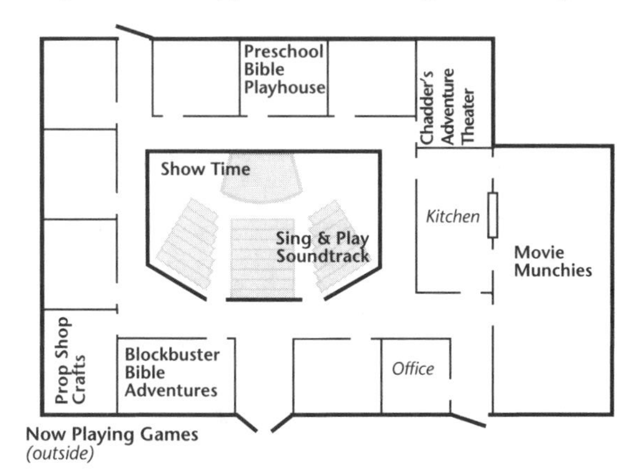

If you have more than 150 kids, your church might be set up like this...

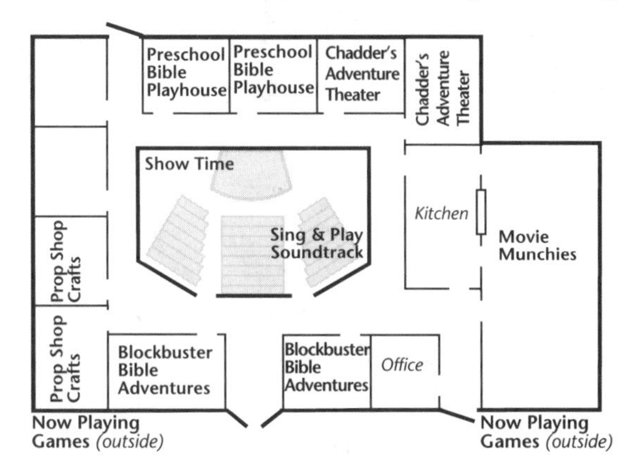

HolyWord HiNtS

For another large-group option, run a morning and evening program. Simply have participants sign up for the daytime or evening program; then decorate once and run two "shifts."

HolyWord HiNtS

Don't worry if you need to set up duplicate Locations—it's easy! If at all possible, place the duplicate Locations next to each other. Then, when Film Crews arrive at the stations, Location Leaders can simply direct half of them into each site.

What's a Film Crew?

As you set up your HolyWord Studios program, you assign kids to Film Crews. On Day 1, kids report to their Film Crews right away to start getting acquainted. Since Film Crew members work closely during the week, Film Crews encourage kids to make new friends at HolyWord Studios. They also provide an organizational structure that helps kids progress from Location to Location in an orderly manner.

Film Crews consist of three to five children and an adult or teenage Film Crew Leader. If you're expecting visitors or want to encourage outreach, assign three children to each Film Crew. Then encourage children to invite their friends to "fill up" their crews. If your attendance is pretty steady, assign up to five children to each crew.

HolyWord HINTS

Try to structure your Film Crews so they contain no more than six members. Through field testing and customer feedback, we've discovered that larger crews can get unmanageable and become a frustration for the crew leader.

If possible, assign one child from each age level to each crew. "Your Film Crew 'Family' " (p. 25), a developmental chart and illustrations, highlights the unique contribution children from each age level can make to a Film Crew. The "Who's Who on the Crew?" chart on page 26 lists the five jobs Film Crew members may fill during HolyWord Studios.

Preschoolers' Film Crews consist of up to five preschoolers and an adult or teenage crew leader.

Detailed instructions for setting up Film Crews begin on page 141. Qualifications for crew leaders are listed on page 97.

HolyWord HINTS

Important! Be sure to distribute the "For Film Crew Leaders Only" handouts (pp. 118-123) to all crew leaders during your leader training time. Have extra handouts available at HolyWord Studios for crew leaders who are unable to attend leader training. These handouts are a *valuable* source of helpful information to those who will work closely with children!

Your Film Crew "Family"

I just finished third grade. I'm a unique and important part of my Film Crew because I like to be challenged. I can help younger members of my Film Crew with challenging projects.

I just finished fifth grade. I'm a unique and important part of my Film Crew because I like to make choices. I can help my Film Crew make choices about a crew name, jobs, and activities.

I just finished second grade. I'm a unique and important part of my Film Crew because I want everything to be fair. I can help make sure we all take turns and treat each other fairly.

I just finished first grade. I'm a unique and important part of my Film Crew because I like to be the best. I can help encourage my Film Crew to be the best it can be.

I just finished kindergarten. I'm a unique and important part of my Film Crew because I have a great imagination. I can help my Film Crew pretend we're really at a big-time movie studio.

I just finished fourth grade. I'm a unique and important part of my Film Crew because I like to ask questions. I can help my Film Crew ask questions to make sure we understand what we're learning.

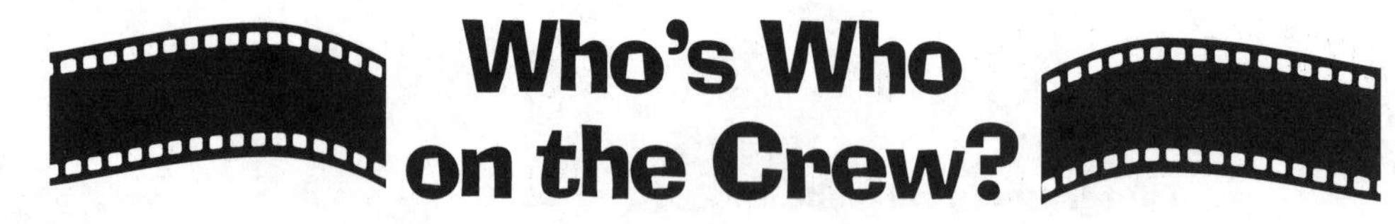

Who's Who on the Crew?

HolyWord HiNtS

As VBS Director, you'll find that open, clear communication is your best friend! Be sure to touch base with the Sing & Play Soundtrack Leader to remind him or her to allow time for children to choose their roles on Day 1. Although this process is written into the Sing & Play Soundtrack Leader Manual, it's good to double-check and be sure the leader understands the importance of this process.

During Sing & Play Soundtrack on Day 1, kids choose Film Crew jobs and place job stickers (from the HolyWord Studios sticker sheets) on their name badges. You can expect each of the following jobs to be represented in each Film Crew. If crews have fewer than five kids, some kids may have more than one job.

In addition to the five jobs listed below, each crew should have an adult or teenage crew leader. You can count on the crew leader to help kids complete the activities at each Location.

Kids are excited about having special jobs! Each leader manual suggests ways Location Leaders can call on kids to fulfill the job responsibilities they've chosen.

Jobs	Duties
Reader	• likes to read • reads Bible passages aloud
Studio Guide	• chooses action ideas for traveling between Locations (such as shuffling, skipping, hopping, galloping, or marching) • helps monitor the daily schedule to let the Film Crew know what's coming next
Materials Manager	• likes to pass out and collect supplies • passes out and collects Student Books • carries the crew's bag until the day is over
Cheerleader	• likes to smile and make people happy • makes sure people use kind words and actions • leads group in cheering during Now Playing Games
Prayer Person	• likes to pray and isn't afraid to pray aloud • makes sure the group takes time to pray each day • leads or opens prayer times

HolyWord HiNtS

Each Film Crew will need one Film Crew bag in which to carry its Student Books, Bible highlighters, Operation Kid-to-Kid items, and crafts. Film Crew bags are available from Group Publishing and your local Christian bookstore.

Where Do Middle Schoolers Fit In?

Many churches are unsure how to handle upper-elementary kids; they seem too old for some children's ministry programs and too young for youth group. With HolyWord Studios, upper-elementary kids can fill a number of roles. (In fact, middle schoolers at our field test reported that they loved helping because it gave them a chance to be an adult...*and* be a kid!) Check out the following options to find the perfect fit for your middle schoolers. They can

- **join Film Crews as Assistant Film Crew Leaders.** Many upper-elementary kids are ready for simple leadership roles, but they still enjoy participating in activities such as games, snack time, crafts, and biblical dramas. As Assistant Film Crew Leaders, they can help their crew leaders by keeping kids together, working with younger children during Prop Shop Crafts, or doing the more difficult jobs during Movie Munchies service.
- **become Assistant Location Leaders.** Your middle schoolers are developing their gifts and talents and are discovering the things they excel at and enjoy. Being an Assistant Location Leader is a great way to encourage kids toward this discovery. Do you know an older child who's developing a love for drama and storytelling? Use him or her as an Assistant Show Time Leader or an Assistant Blockbuster Bible Adventures Leader. What about a child who enjoys sports and other athletic activities? Ask him or her to be an Assistant Now Playing Games Leader. Your Location Leaders will love the extra help, and older kids will enjoy the added responsibility.
- **help with Preschool Bible Playhouse registration.** Some middle schoolers are nurturing and caring—great qualities for helping preschoolers find their way at HolyWord Studios. For the first day or two, have a few middle schoolers available to act as "tour guides," helping preschoolers find their Film Crew Leaders, showing preschoolers the restroom, or playing with a shy child to get him or her accustomed to Preschool Bible Playhouse.
- **create an upper-elementary Sing-Along Crew.** Older children (who might normally hesitate to sing and move to music) will enjoy teaching song motions and leading younger children in Sing & Play Soundtrack. Ask a group of upper-elementary kids to work with the Sing & Play Soundtrack Leader to learn the words and motions to all thirteen HolyWord Studios songs. The Sing-Along Crew will add visual excitement and energy to your singing time.

Middle schoolers have so much to offer (and gain from) your program! We've heard countless stories of middle schoolers and teenagers whose lives were changed because of their experience in leading or assisting in VBS. The more these kids are involved in your program, the more opportunities you have to touch their lives.

A Cue From Our Crew

It's important that middle school kids understand the specifics of their jobs. We discovered that assigning kids this age as "Floaters" who could fill in wherever there was a need gave them too much freedom and not enough direction. When we gave them specific roles, such as Assistant Chef or Assistant Prop Shop Crafts Leader, they did a super job of helping out!

A Cue From Our Crew

Make sure you choose more mature fifth- and sixth-graders for leadership roles. Many kids this age still enjoy being crew members and participating in all activities. In our field test, we assumed that one fifth-grade boy would make a great preschool crew leader. As it turned out, he felt slighted because he couldn't make his own cool craft or participate fully in other activities. Be sure to ask kids what they'd like to do instead of assuming they'd rather opt "out."

A Cue From Our Crew

Who says VBS is just for little kids? We've heard so many stories of how teenagers' lives were touched by past VBS programs. Young adults who volunteered had such a great time and were so moved by the Bible experiences, they made life-changing decisions!

A Cue From Our Crew

We asked the teenagers at our VBS if they missed having their own high school class, with activities designed just for them. Not one *of these young adults felt like they missed out by not having "youth group" VBS! "We get to be with kids our own age all year...this was a chance for us to do something different and help with the little kids." Plus, these teenagers absolutely loved the hugs and love lavished on them by the kids.*

HolyWord HiNtS

We've heard from churches who allowed their youth to choose the material then run the entire program as their summer outreach or service project! It's a super way to involve young people in real hands-on ministry!

Do Teenagers Have a Role at HolyWord Studios?

Teenagers have an important role in making HolyWord Studios a successful production! Use the following suggestions to involve teenagers (or college students) in your program:

- **Have them act as Film Crew Leaders.** Many young adults have younger siblings or baby-sit frequently and are comfortable working with children. Young adults will have a great time leading their crews—and will love how easy it is. (Teenagers will actually get as much out of the Bible stories and discussions as the young children will!)
- **Let teenagers and young adults help with registration.** Believe it or not, some young people have excellent organizational skills. These young people enjoy forming crews, greeting children, and helping kids find their Film Crew Leaders. (These "ushers" make a great first impression for adults as well as kids!) After the first day, your registration helpers can register newcomers, count the daily attendance and report the number to the Movie Munchies Leader, and fill in for crew leaders who are absent.
- **Have qualified teenagers run your sound system or act as photographers.** Some high school drama programs train young people how to run sound, lighting, and video equipment. These teenagers make excellent HolyWord Studios technical staff members. You may even ask them to put together a slide show or video production of your program!
- **Ask teenagers to act as Blockbuster Bible Adventures volunteers.** The Blockbuster Bible Adventures Leader needs several volunteers to act as Bible characters in simple dramas. Teenagers with dramatic flair enjoy playing an Egyptian guard, Pharaoh's daughter, or Pharaoh.
- **If your church's youth group has a choir or worship band, let it help with Sing & Play Soundtrack and Show Time.** Kids at HolyWord Studios love singing with the "big kids," and young adults will never have such a receptive and friendly audience again! Your Location Leaders enjoy the extra backup and enthusiasm. Plus teenagers learn and grow right along with the children!

There are countless ways to involve youth in HolyWord Studios. Just let teenagers find roles where their gifts, talents, or interests lead them! You'll be surprised at how committed and enthusiastic these young volunteers are.

What's a Student Book?

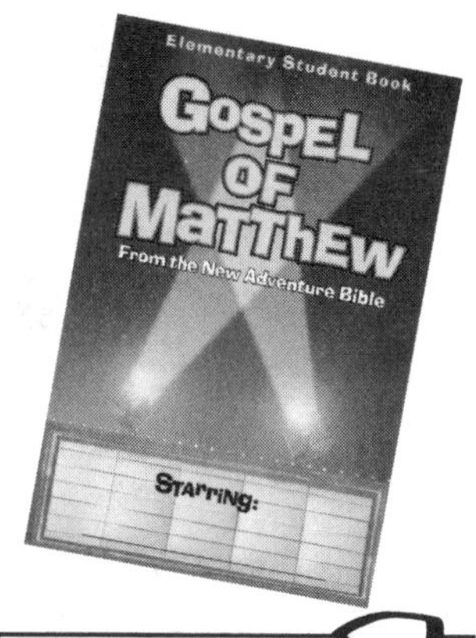

Each child at HolyWord Studios will need a Student Book. The Student Book is the Gospel of Matthew, taken from The New Adventure Bible. This easy-to-understand Bible translation is filled with age-appropriate study helps, interesting Bible facts, and short devotional thoughts. Kids will dig in to practical Bible study skills—learning how to read, highlight, and create helpful tabs for finding important verses long after VBS.

Each Student Book also contains four specially designed bandages. Kids will need two of the bandages for Operation Kid-to-Kid, an international service project that links kids in North America with children around the world. During the week, kids at your VBS will collect important items such as soap, a washcloth, a toothbrush, and toothpaste (see page 41 for more details). Then, at the end of the week, each Film Crew will place all the items in an Operation Kid-to-Kid resealable plastic bag to create a Care Kit. Film Crews will present the Care Kits as an offering at Show Time. You can give the kits to a needy church in your area, donate them to a local mission or shelter, or send the packets to Operation Mobilization for worldwide distribution. For more information on Operation Mobilization, check out page 40 of this manual. This is a meaningful, hands-on way for kids to share God's love with others.

Preschoolers have their own age-appropriate Student Books, each complete with five illustrated Bible stories and four activity pages to make Bible learning fun and memorable. Preschoolers' parents will appreciate the take-home newsletters—full of easy follow-up ideas, fun Bible-learning songs, and simple crafts that reinforce each day's Bible story and Point.

Preschoolers will look forward to adding stickers to their Bible books, just like the "big kids." They'll even create their own Care Kits, proving that you're never too young to share God's love!

A Cue From Our Crew

In field-testing the Student Books, we tried having children use an entire New Testament. This proved a little confusing for younger children, who occasionally found the correct chapter and verse...in the wrong Bible book! Make Bible exploration simple and successful by providing a "kid-sized bite" of the Bible for each child. One book of the Bible is just right for kids to work with.

HolyWord Hints

You'll want to provide a HolyWord Studios sticker sheet for each child (elementary and preschool) at your VBS. These sticker sheets include all the stickers kids will need for crafts and for their Student Books. Kids will love the bright, fun designs, and you'll *love* finding everything in one place!

Who Is Chadder Chipmunk™?

Chadder Chipmunk is a lovable, mischievous character the kids love. Each day when kids visit Chadder's Adventure Theater, they view a segment of *Chadder's HolyWord Adventure.*

Kids enjoy a time-machine adventure with Chadder, where Chadder discovers that the Bible is like a script, directing us through life. Though children of all ages laugh at Chadder's antics as he stumbles through Bible times, they also discover important Bible truths that apply to everyday life.

Chadder the chipmunk explains that he's getting ready to make a movie about a chipmunk who travels back to Bible times. Suddenly, the "fake" time machine really works, transporting Chadder back to the day that baby Moses was pulled from the Nile. Chadder meets Carmine the Camel, and convinces Carmine that God cares for Moses, since Chadder knows the outcome of the story from his Bible. Next, the two travel through time to see Moses confronting Pharaoh during the plagues. They meet Hoppy, a gloomy frog who explains that God protected the Israelites from awful things like darkness and bugs. As the three travelers cross the Red Sea with the Israelites, they hear that God loved his people so much that he kept them from death during Passover. After a near miss in the Red Sea, Chadder and his friends escape, only to find themselves transported to Jerusalem. The travelers talk with a saddened Mary, distraught after Jesus' death. Chadder reassures everyone that his script—the Bible—tells that Jesus rises from the dead. Chadder explains that Jesus was like the Passover lamb, saving us all from death. The last time-leap lands Chadder and his friends in Jerusalem during Pentecost, where they see the birth of the church. Suddenly, Chadder is hit on the head and awakes, realizing that his adventure was really a dream. Fortunately, he remembers that the Bible is real, and God's story is better than any movie!

The Chadder's Adventure Theater Leader Manual contains discussion questions that go along with each day's segment of *Chadder's HolyWord Adventure.* The video is available from Group Publishing and your local Christian bookstore.

HolyWord HiNtS

Your kids will love Chadder and will look forward to seeing him! Not only will they enjoy the twists and turns of the story, but they'll appreciate the wonderful downtime during a busy day at HolyWord Studios. Kids are so active during VBS that it's nice for them to have a few moments to sit down, cool off, and take five! (Your Film Crew Leaders will appreciate it, too!)

A Cue From Our Crew

Kids really loved Chadder! They sang along, applauded, giggled, and pleaded for more of the show each day! Because it left them wanting more, it turned out to be a great attendance-builder from day to day!

Can Kids *Really* Make Their Own Snacks

Each day at HolyWord Studios, a different group of kids skips their Now Playing Games time so they can prepare snacks for the entire VBS. Snack preparation provides kids a unique opportunity to live out the daily Bible Point by serving others. And it makes your job easier because you don't have to recruit additional volunteers to make snacks.

Believe it or not, one-fourth of your kids *can* prepare snacks for everyone else—if you follow the field-tested, step-by-step instructions provided in the Movie Munchies Leader Manual. Each day, snack preparation will follow the simple procedures outlined below.

1. Before kids arrive, the Movie Munchies Leader sets out supplies according to the diagrams provided in the Movie Munchies Leader Manual.

2. After kids arrive and wash their hands, the leader explains each step of the snack preparation and invites kids to choose which steps they'd like to work on.

3. Kids work in assembly lines to prepare the snacks. Film Crew Leaders are assigned the more difficult tasks such as handling sharp knives or pouring drinks.

4. Kids set out the completed snacks on tables, where they'll be picked up and gobbled down during Movie Munchies.

Kids who serve on the Movie Munchies Service Crew report for snack preparation right after Sing & Play Soundtrack. They'll take twenty to twenty-five minutes to prepare snacks before moving on to their next Location. And just in case kids don't finish in time, the Movie Munchies Leader has an additional twenty to twenty-five minutes to make final preparations before all the children arrive to eat. In HolyWord Studios field tests, even preschoolers were able to complete their snack preparation within the allotted time!

As Studio Director, you'll want to drop in on the Movie Munchies Service Crew each day. Ask the leader how kids' work is progressing, and affirm the children for a job well done. But don't linger too long; you may distract kids from completing their work. Be sure to return at snack time to see children explain the meaning of the snack as *they* teach the Bible Point. Then watch the Movie Munchies Service Crew kids' faces light up as they're recognized for their accomplishment!

A Cue From Our Crew

"Kids won't want to give up their game time just to make snacks!" Think again! In our field test, Movie Munchies Service became something kids really looked forward to. At the end of each day's Sing & Play Soundtrack, the HolyWord Studios Director would announce which group would be preparing the snack that day. You could hear the "lucky" kids whisper, "Yeah!" "All right!" or "That's us!" within their crews. We think it was terrific that kids looked forward to serving others.

OPERATION
Kid-to-Kid™
Sharing God's Love
Around the World

What Is Operation Kid-to-Kid™?

More Than an Offering

In developing HolyWord Studios, the VBS team at Group Publishing wanted to include a meaningful service project to help kids realize that with God's help, even children can impact the world! We know that kids today are service-minded and want to make a difference, both globally and within their communities. From customer feedback, we learned that VBS Directors (like you) wanted kids to give more than money. They wanted kids to give something that was meaningful and tangible—something that would meet the needs of children across the world.

We contacted Operation Mobilization, an interdenominational mission organization with a passion for reaching the world with the good news of God's love. Operation Mobilization's two mission ships serve people in countries from Albania to Uruguay. In fact, since 1971, their ships have welcomed 26 million people in more than 400 cities in 131 nations! In the process, they've distributed more than 17 million Christian and educational books and more than 1.5 million Bibles and New Testaments.

We could see that Operation Mobilization certainly knew the needs of children around the world. One of the needs they identified was for simple, basic hygiene items—a toothbrush, a bar of soap, and a washcloth, for example. Without such basic items, children in poverty-stricken areas can develop health and medical problems that can oftentimes become serious. By providing simple Care Kits, children in North America can help meet the basic needs of children around the world. So we've partnered with Operation Mobilization to develop a meaningful, hands-on missions project that will allow the kids at your church to reach children across the globe.

> **A Cue From Our Crew**
> *As we hear reports from past Operation Kid-to-Kid programs, we've been humbled at how God works!* The success of these programs is mind-boggling—*especially when you consider the widespread international reach that kids right here in North America are having. This is a phenomenal way to help kids understand that they* can *make a difference!*

How Your Kids Can Help

First of all, determine where you'll focus your mission. In past years, some VBS Directors let us know that they wanted a service project that would affect children right in their own communities. Others preferred a more international project. Operation Kid-to-Kid is easy to adapt for any situation. So choose where you'll send the Care Kits; then get kids excited about the need they'll meet.

Each Film Crew will put together a Care Kit containing the items pictured on page

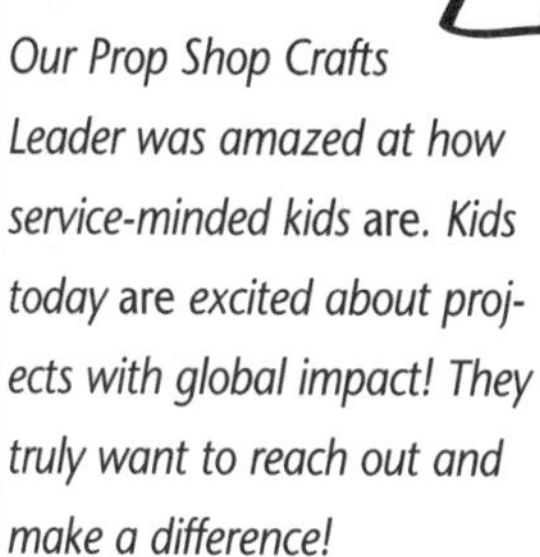

> **A Cue From Our Crew**
> *Our Prop Shop Crafts Leader was amazed at how service-minded kids* are. *Kids* today *are excited about projects with global impact! They truly want to reach out and make a difference!*

41. On Day 2 of Prop Shop Crafts, Film Crew members will work together to decide who will bring in which items. Children will then circle the items they are bringing on their Operation Kid-to-Kid newsletters (found on page 47-48 of their Student Books). Since there is a total of seven items and since we've provided the bandages, each child will need to bring in only one of the items on the list. (We suggest that the Film Crew Leader bring in the one dollar, which will be used to add foreign-language Bible materials to each kit. Canadian participants will need to add two Canadian dollars.) We've given each child four specially printed bandages in the Student Book. Children may take two of the bandages home, then add two to the Care Kit for a total of ten bandages in each Kit. If parents can't provide an item, they'll circle the last paragraph on the handout and return it to you. For this reason, you'll need to have a few extra items on hand to fill in some packs. (Check out the ideas on page 38 to decide how your church and community members can provide the extras.)

On Day 5, the kids will use the resealable bags from the Starter Kit. (Even the plastic bag has a purpose! Kids in needy countries can use the bag to carry clean water.) Children will create their Operation Kid-to-Kid Care Kits in Prop Shop Crafts. They'll also work together to create a special card for the recipient. Then, children will keep the Care Kits with them until Show Time. During the closing program, Film Crews will bring their Care Kits forward as an offering to God. This is a powerful, moving ceremony. Kids and leaders will be amazed as they watch the "mountain" of gifts grow higher and higher. It's a very concrete way for kids to see that we all have an important part in God's amazing story.

A Cue From Our Crew

"Kids will really complain if they can't make a craft on Day 5!" We wondered that, too. After all, the crafts at HolyWord Studios are a huge hit. But not one child (of our 150 elementary kids) complained or even noticed! They were so excited to create their Care Kits and design special cards that they didn't mind going without a craft for one day. We were truly touched by their selfless and serving attitudes!

After your HolyWord Studios production "wraps," it's time to distribute your Care Kits. Here are a few options:

• Have families deliver them, door-to-door, to needy families in or near your community.

• Have children take them to a homeless shelter in or near your community. Allow the kids to play Now Playing Games, lead Sing & Play Soundtrack songs, watch the *Chadder's HolyWord Adventure* video, and enjoy Movie Munchies together.

A Cue From Our Crew

We discovered that kids need a small-group setting to discuss, understand, and focus on Operation Kid-to-Kid. Prop Shop Crafts is a natural "Operation Kid-to-Kid Headquarters." There, children learn about the project and its impact, and create the Care Kits and Care Kit cards. In Prop Shop Crafts, kids also "meet" three children (through Operation Kid-to-Kid posters) who are representatives of the children who will receive the Care Kits.

• Send the kits along with your youth (or another group) on a missions trip. This is a super way for your kids to support a missions team in a tangible way.

• Send the kits to Operation Mobilization for worldwide distribution. Take out the dollar bill from each individual Care Kit, then write a check to Operation Mobilization for the total amount. (So they don't receive cash, which isn't as secure to send.) They'll use the funds to include foreign-language Bible literature in each Care Kit. Then simply place the packs in a large, sturdy box and tape it shut. Affix the mailing label from the Operation Kid-to-Kid brochure (in the Starter Kit), add your church address and the number of kits included, then ship the box to the Kid-to-Kid Send-Off Center. In the United States, mail your package to:

OM Literature
129 Mobilization Drive
Waynesboro, GA 30830

In Canada, mail your package to:
OM Canada
212 West Street
Port Colborne
Ontario L3K 4E3

Operation Kid-to-Kid Countdown

Two Months Before HolyWord Studios

• **Inform your congregation.** Photocopy the "We're Taking Our HolyWord Studios Production Across the Globe!" bulletin insert (p. 41), and distribute it at a worship service. This handout explains Operation Kid-to-Kid and lets church members know how they can help.

• **Involve your congregation.** Church members can help by providing the extra items you'll need if kids aren't able to or forget to bring their items. This is a super way to involve church members who can't give their time to HolyWord Studios.

✔ Set a box in the church office to collect extra items to help fill the Care Kits. Encourage church members to check the list in the bulletin and donate whatever items they can.

✔ Check with your college group, singles group, or senior citizens group to see if they'd be interested in trying to fill a small box with extra Care Kit items. (Remember, the items must be the same ones on the list.)

✔ Take a special offering to collect money to buy the necessary items. You can also use this money for shipping costs.

• **Involve your community.** Check with local discount stores or grocery stores to see if they would be willing to donate basic hygiene items for Operation Kid-to-Kid. They may actually donate enough items that children won't need to bring anything! You could also ask the stores to provide supplies for children whose families are unable to purchase items.

• **Consider setting up an Operation Kid-to-Kid "store"** if you live in a rural area where kids might have trouble getting these items on short notice. Gather enough items (from church members and donations from local merchants) for each Film Crew to make a Care Kit. During HolyWord Studios, display the items in a corner of your church. Allow children to purchase the item they've chosen using real money or "mission money" you've distributed.

Two Weeks Before HolyWord Studios

• **Distribute supplemental supplies.** Give Operation Kid-to-Kid bags (from the Starter Kit) to the Preschool Bible Playhouse Director and Prop Shop Crafts Leader. Each of these leaders will also need the three Operation Kid-to-Kid posters, available from Group Publishing and your local Christian bookstore.

• **Publicize your project.** Photocopy the "Operation Kid-to-Kid News Release" on page 42, and fill in the information regarding your church's program. Send the news release to local newspapers, television, and radio stations so they can let others in your community know about your participation in Operation Kid-to-Kid.

HolyWord HiNtS

A picture really is worth a thousand words! The Operation Kid-to-Kid posters help kids connect the face of a child to this project. By posting these pictures for kids to see, you help Operation Kid-to-Kid take on a more personal feeling for kids. It's a great way to build enthusiasm and make outreach meaningful.

During HolyWord Studios

• **Remind kids to bring their items.** When the Sing & Play Soundtrack Leader or the Show Time Leader calls you up to make announcements, encourage kids to bring their items before Day 5.

• **Remind kids of the importance of their mission.** Often, kids in North America take basic hygiene items for granted. Talk about what it would be like to never brush your teeth or to have dirty hands all the time. Let them think about how they could carry clean water if they didn't have a clean bowl or pitcher. Remind kids that these Care Kits are an easy way to show God's love and care to kids around the world.

• **Affirm kids when they accomplish their role.** Each day, lead kids in cheering for those who've brought their hygiene supplies. This positive reinforcement will be more powerful than all the nagging in the world!

• **Check in with Film Crew Leaders.** During your opening huddle and prayer with Film Crew Leaders, ask them how well their Operation Kid-to-Kid items are coming in. This will give you a feel for the number of extra items you might need at the end of the week.

• **Encourage kids to pray for their "Care Kit Kids."** During Sing & Play Soundtrack or in Show Time, allow a short time for kids to pray for the children who will receive the Care Kits. Children can pray that the recipients (or their "Care Kit Kids") will sense how much God cares for them, through this simple act.

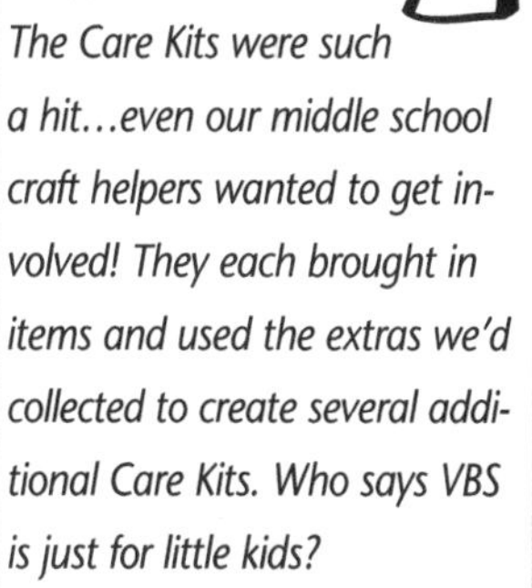

The Care Kits were such a hit...even our middle school craft helpers wanted to get involved! They each brought in items and used the extras we'd collected to create several additional Care Kits. Who says VBS is just for little kids?

After HolyWord Studios

• **Send your Care Kits to the Kid-to-Kid Send-Off Center.** Collect the dollar bills from each Care Kit, then write one check for the total amount to Operation Mobilization. Place your Care Kits in a large, sturdy packing box. Tape the box shut, and affix

the mailing label from the Operation Kid-to-Kid brochure in your Starter Kit. Be sure to include your church address on the package, as well as the number of kits you're sending.

• **Look for your Operation Kid-to-Kid update.** If you choose to send your Care Kits to Operation Mobilization, OM will send your church a newsletter about Operation Kid-to-Kid several months after your program. You'll learn how this outreach program affected thousands of children around the world. Share this powerful information with your children; they'll love hearing that their Care Kits went around the world to spread God's love and care!

• **Remind kids to visit the Operation Kid-to-Kid Web site.** Technology today will allow kids to chat with other Operation Kid-to-Kid participants and learn more about the countries where the kits may be sent. Children will enjoy visiting the Operation Kid-to-Kid Web site (www.OK2K.org).

We're Taking Our HolyWord Studios Production Around the Globe!

At HolyWord Studios, not only will your kids star in God's story, they'll take the news of God's amazing love and share it with children around the world. This hands-on mission project, called Operation Kid-to-Kid™, will allow kids in North America to create and send Care Kits to needy children around the globe. The Care Kits contain basic hygiene items to help less fortunate children get healthy and stay healthy.

Each Film Crew (a group of five children and a Film Crew Leader who participate together in HolyWord Studios activities) will create one Care Kit containing the **new** items listed below. Kids will work with their Film Crews to decide who will bring which items. The Care Kit items are:

a bath-sized bar of soap

a four- to six-ounce tube of toothpaste

a washcloth

a comb

a one-dollar bill (or two Canadian dollars)

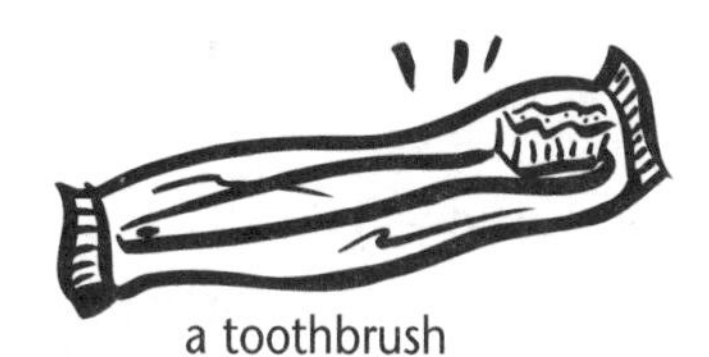
a toothbrush

bandages

The adhesive bandages for the kits are included in the children's Student Books. **If your child will be attending HolyWord Studios, please wait to find out what he or she has chosen to bring before purchasing any items!** If you would like to donate extra items, please feel free to do so. We'll need extras for children who are unable to bring their own.

Contact ______________________ at ______________________ for more information.
VBS Director / Phone number

Operation Kid-to Kid™ News Release

Adapt the information in this news release to fit your church's HolyWord Studios production. Then submit typed, double-spaced copies to your local newspapers, radio stations, and TV stations. You may want to check with them for any other specific requirements regarding news releases.

A Cue From Our Crew

When we sent our news release to the local paper, the newspaper printed it as "Holywood Studios." Although our copy was correct, the editor at the paper must have thought we'd made a mistake. Be sure to add a note that your title is "HolyWord" not "Holywood." It's a way to bring attention to the Bible, God's Holy Word!

[Name of church] will be involved in a worldwide mission project called Operation Kid-to-Kid™. For this project, children attending [name of church]'s HolyWord Studios vacation Bible school will send Care Kits (containing basic hygiene items) to children around the world.

Operation Kid-to-Kid will show kids that, even though we're separated by language and distance, everyone can share God's love! Kids in North America will design special cards to include in the Care Kits. The Care Kits will be shipped to Operation Mobilization, who will distribute them to children in countries around the world. Past Operation Kid-to-Kid programs have allowed nearly a million children in North America to send thousands of school supplies and Spanish-translations of the Gospel of John to children around the world.

Operation Kid-to-Kid is just one part of HolyWord Studios, a program in which kids star in God's story. HolyWord Studios begins production [starting date] and continues through [ending date]. It's located at [name of church and church address]. Registration opens each day at [starting time] and closes at [ending time]. For more information, call [church phone number].

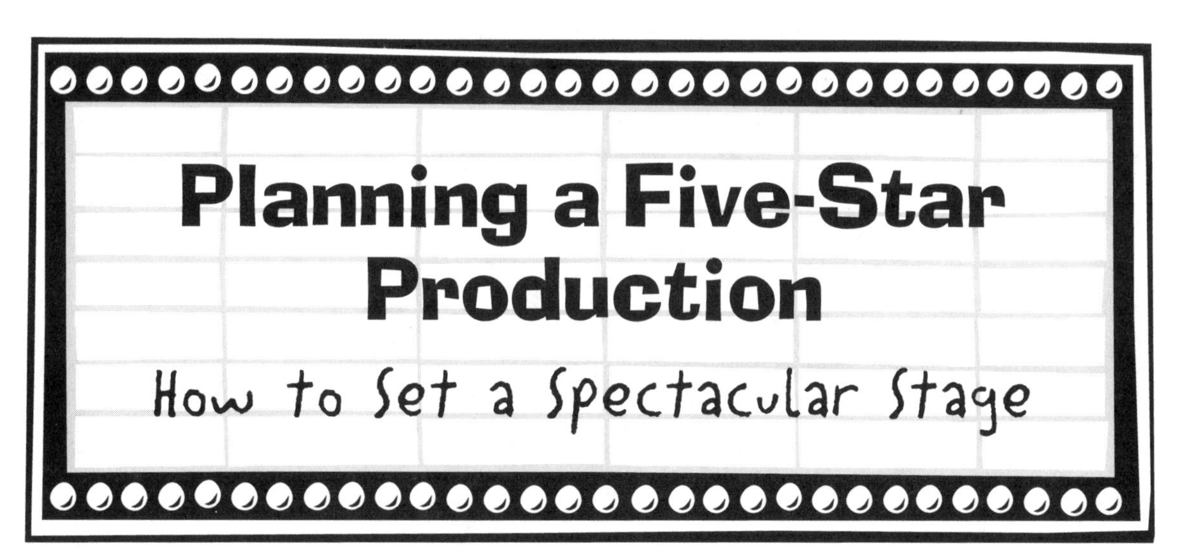
Planning a Five-Star Production
How to Set a Spectacular Stage

Planning Calendar

Three to Six Months Before HolyWord Studios

☆ **Begin praying for your church's HolyWord Studios.** Ask God to prepare the hearts of church members, workers, and children who will attend.

☆ **Choose a format for your HolyWord Studios.**

- ✔ Will you meet in the morning or in the evening?
- ✔ Will you meet every day for a week or once a week for several weeks?
- ✔ Will your program be for children only or will entire families be invited to attend?
- ✔ Will you meet at your church or another location?

☆ **Set HolyWord Studios dates.** As you're considering dates, you may want to find out about other summer programs offered by your church or your community so you can avoid conflicts.

☆ **Choose a Studio Director.** If you're reading this manual, that's you! The director is responsible for planning, recruiting staff, and overseeing all details to ensure that HolyWord Studios goes smoothly.

☆ **Set a budget.** Your church may already include VBS in its budget. If so, find out what funds are available. If your church doesn't have a VBS budget in place, consider the following ideas:

- ✔ Collect an offering to cover expenses.
- ✔ Charge a per-child registration fee for HolyWord Studios. Give discounts to families that register more than one child.
- ✔ Invite congregation members to "sponsor" children by contributing a per-child amount. (See the "Registration" section on pages 137-154 for more specifics on this idea.)
- ✔ Hold a creative fund-raiser! Host a "HolyWord Premiere Night" to show a family movie. (*The Muppet Movie* is a fun, thematic film that all ages will enjoy.) Sell traditional-looking tickets, movie-style popcorn, and snacks such as Good & Plenty or Junior Mints. Or open your own "Planet HolyWord" and serve a simple dinner. Have volunteers dress as "stars"—such as Cecil B. DeMovie (an over-the-top director), Sylvester Cyclone (a large action star), and Greta Garbage (a melodramatic actress)—who serve the food or perform

HolyWord HiNtS

We frequently hear back from customers who hold a very "nontraditional" VBS—using different settings, times, or dates. Be creative and choose the best VBS setting for your church situation!

short skits or songs for entertainment. Not only will this raise funds for your program, it will get everyone excited about your HolyWord Studios!

A Cue From Our Crew

"Our VBS has grown so much—we're almost out of room!" We've heard it from customers, and it's even happening to us! Our first VBS field test averaged about seventy-five kids per day. This summer we averaged two hundred children each day! Wow! We're delighted that God's story is spreading to so many children in our community!

Two to Three Months Before HolyWord Studios

☆ **Plan HolyWord Studios publicity.** Decide how you'll promote HolyWord Studios in your church and community. Refer to the "Publicity: Getting Two Thumbs Up From Your Church and Community" section (pp. 125-136) in this manual for publicity ideas and resources.

☆ **Begin recruiting Location Leaders.** Photocopy the leader job descriptions (pp. 89-96). Give the job descriptions to people in your church who'd enjoy leading a Location. Or post the job descriptions on a large bulletin board you've covered with movie posters or trimmed with perforated film edging. As you talk to people, focus on the job descriptions rather than on previous church teaching experience. A restaurant chef who's never taught Sunday school might make a great Movie Munchies Leader! We've heard from lots of VBS Directors who say that this program is a great way to involve people who don't think they have anything to offer children! (And once they've tried it, they're hooked!)

You might want to announce your staffing needs in a worship service. Then post the job descriptions on a large sheet of poster board under the heading "Casting Call: You Can Have a Starring Role in the Life of a Child." People can sign their names on the job descriptions they're interested in. It's OK if more than one person signs up for each Location. Team teaching is the way to go!

A Cue From Our Crew

***Important!** As we've said, people who have used Group's VBS in the past tell us their VBS programs are growing! To avoid stress and disappointment, order early and order extras!*

☆ **Estimate your HolyWord Studios enrollment.** Use figures from your church's Sunday school or figures from last year's VBS program. Once you've estimated how many children will attend, figure out how many Film Crew Leaders you'll need. You'll need one adult or teenage Film Crew Leader for every five children, including preschoolers. Be sure to have extra Film Crew Leaders ready in case you need to form Film Crews from last-minute registrants.

☆ **Order HolyWord Studios materials.** If you purchased the HolyWord Studios Starter Kit, you already have a leader manual for every Location. You may want to order additional leader manuals for team teaching. Your Chadder's Adventure Theater Leader will need a copy of the *Chadder's HolyWord Adventure* video.

For every elementary-age child, you'll *need* to order

✔ an Elementary Student Book;
✔ an elementary HolyWord Studios sticker sheet; and
✔ craft items:

★ one TLSeed Necklace container,
★ one Yahoo Yo-Yo and yo-yo string,
★ one Incredi-Ball powder packet, and
★ one Amazing Picture.

For every preschooler, you'll *need* to order

- ✔ a Preschool Student Book;
- ✔ a preschool HolyWord Studios sticker sheet; and
- ✔ craft items:
  - ★ one TLSeed Necklace container,
  - ★ one Cool Cap
  - ★ one Magnificent Megaphone,
  - ★ one All-Star Frame, and
  - ★ two or three puffy stars.

Even if you're planning a late-summer program, it's not too early to order materials! As you update your registration count, you can order additional student supplies as needed.

☆ **"Scout" your church facilities.** Just as real location scouts check out the best background for a movie to be shot, you'll want to be deliberate in selecting your Location areas. You'll need to set up a separate room or area for each site. Use the following guidelines:

☆ **Sing & Play Soundtrack**

- ✔ large room to accommodate the entire cast and crew (possibly a sanctuary or fellowship hall)
- ✔ sound system/microphone (helpful)
- ✔ outlet to plug in audiocassette player or CD player (or a sound system to play *Sing & Play Soundtrack* audiocassette or CD)
- ✔ outlet to plug in overhead projector (if using *Sing & Play Soundtrack Transparencies*)

☆ **Chadder's Adventure Theater**

- ✔ classroom to accommodate all the preschoolers at once and to accommodate one-fourth of the elementary-age kids (helpful if room can be darkened)
- ✔ outlet to plug in TV/VCR

☆ **Prop Shop Crafts**

- ✔ classroom to accommodate one-fourth of the elementary-age kids
- ✔ one or two low tables (helpful)
- ✔ outlet to plug in audiocassette player or CD player if using *Sing & Play Soundtrack* audiocassette or CD

☆ **Movie Munchies**

- ✔ large room to accommodate entire HolyWord Studios cast and crew (possibly a fellowship hall or gymnasium)
- ✔ church kitchen or other noncarpeted area for Movie Munchies Service

☆ **Now Playing Games**

- ✔ room or outdoor area to accommodate one-fourth of the elementary-age kids (a fellowship hall, gymnasium, or lawn)
- ✔ room enough for children to run around
- ✔ outlet to plug in audiocassette player or CD player if using *Sing & Play Soundtrack* audiocassette or CD

HolyWord HiNtS

If your plans involve more than 150 children, consider running two or more simultaneous Locations. For more information on how to do this, see "What's a Location?" (p. 22).

A Cue From Our Crew

During Prop Shop Crafts, we found that it's easier for children to work on the floor, rather than at tables. (We had set out a tarp, but realized that we didn't need it because the crafts are all no-mess!)

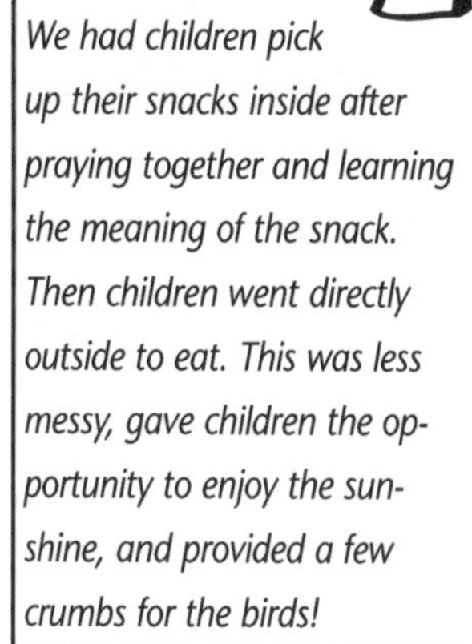

A Cue From Our Crew

We had children pick up their snacks inside after praying together and learning the meaning of the snack. Then children went directly outside to eat. This was less messy, gave children the opportunity to enjoy the sunshine, and provided a few crumbs for the birds!

☆ **Blockbuster Bible Adventures**

- ✔ classroom that can comfortably accommodate one-fourth of the elementary-age kids and that can be darkened
- ✔ classroom that's in a quiet area of your facility (helpful for storytelling, especially on Day 4)
- ✔ outlet to plug in audiocassette player

☆ **Show Time**

- ✔ large room to accommodate entire HolyWord Studios cast and crew (possibly a sanctuary or fellowship hall; could use the same room as Sing & Play Soundtrack)
- ✔ sound system/microphone (helpful)
- ✔ outlet to plug in audiocassette player
- ✔ stage (helpful)

☆ **Preschool Bible Playhouse**

- ✔ classroom(s) to accommodate all preschoolers
- ✔ outlet to plug in audiocassette player
- ✔ restroom facilities in room or nearby
- ✔ child-sized furniture
- ✔ preschool toys such as blocks, modeling dough, dress-up clothes, and stuffed animals

☆ Plan and schedule a leader training meeting using the " 'Lights, Camera, Action!' Leader Training Meeting" (p. 108). This outline incorporates the *Sneak Preview* video, which contains clips from HolyWord Studios field tests. Your Location Leaders will enjoy seeing HolyWord Studios in action. Be sure to include Film Crew Leaders in your training so they can better understand their role. The *Sneak Preview* video includes a section just for crew leaders that explains their duties and describes how to be effective in discussions and with discipline.

Plan to meet for at least two hours.

HolyWord HINTS

Since preschoolers work at learning centers or sites, you may want to set up one room for these sites and use another place for storytelling and singing.

HolyWord HINTS

If you can't arrange for all your leaders to make it to your leader training meeting, consider videotaping the meeting. Send copies of the videotape to volunteers who couldn't make it. If you can't videotape the session, send the *Sneak Preview* video to your leaders to better prepare them for their roles.

Eight Weeks Before HolyWord Studios

☆ **Begin recruiting Film Crew Leaders.** Film Crew Leaders are like older brothers and sisters in the Film Crew family. They aren't responsible for teaching, and they don't have to prepare anything. Film Crew Leaders can be teenagers, college students, parents, or grandparents. They need only to love the Lord and love children.

Film Crew Leaders should plan to participate in HolyWord Studios for the entire "shoot." If they need to be absent one or more days, encourage them to find their own substitutes.

HolyWord HINTS

Although we would encourage Film Crew Leaders to commit to the full time, if they have to bring in a "double," use it to your advantage. Show those substitutes that helping in VBS can be fun! They may even decide to volunteer next year!

☆ **Begin publicity.** Fill in your program's dates and times on the HolyWord Studios outdoor banner (available from Group Publishing and your local Christian bookstore). Display the banner in a prominent outdoor location.

Hang HolyWord Studios theme posters (available from Group Publishing and your local Christian bookstore) in your church and community.

Movie studios show "trailers" (or previews) to get audiences excited about coming attractions. Show the promotional segment of the *Sneak Preview* video during a worship service or other church gathering. This five-minute segment, found at the beginning of your *Sneak Preview* video, shows scenes from actual HolyWord Studios programs. You'll find that the video helps build enthusiasm, recruit volunteers, and promote attendance for your program.

Post the Bible movie posters (available from Group Publishing or your local Christian bookstore) around your church. These humorous, eye-catching posters will help everyone catch the spirit and anticipate a fun-filled production!

☆ **Begin gathering supplies.** Refer to the master supply list, "Supplies: Everything You Need for a Five-Star Production" (p. 61). Consult with Location Leaders to inform them of how you'll handle supply collection. Will you gather all supplies or will each leader gather his or her own supplies? You may want to ask church members to donate food supplies (such as string cheese, pretzel sticks, or cupcakes) or easy-to-find items (such as laundry baskets or old sheets).

☆ **Plan your HolyWord Studios schedule.** The average VBS program runs for up to three hours each day. Group's HolyWord Studios materials have been developed with these parameters in mind. For a three-hour program, Sing & Play Soundtrack and Show Time should last twenty-five minutes apiece, and every other Location should last twenty minutes. See the daily schedules on pages 76-84 to see how this works. If your program will meet for more or less time than three hours each day, you'll need to adapt these times accordingly.

Four Weeks Before HolyWord Studios

☆ **Recruit additional volunteers.** In addition to Location Leaders and Film Crew Leaders, you may want to recruit volunteers to help with registration, transportation, photography, and child care for the staff.

☆ **Continue publicity.** Mail HolyWord Studios invitation postcards to children in your church and community. Distribute HolyWord Studios doorknob danglers in your community. Write your church's name and when your HolyWord Studios will begin.

☆ **Begin preregistration.** Photocopy the "HolyWord Studios Registration

A Cue From Our Crew

We've heard stories of crew leaders who, before VBS, claimed they would have to miss a few days because of other plans. But after experiencing a few days at this VBS, they quickly changed their other plans so they wouldn't miss out!

A Cue From Our Crew

We found that by adding five minutes to Sing & Play Soundtrack and Show Time, the rest of the schedule flowed much more smoothly. It also allowed time for kids to sing extra favorites (and there were plenty of those!).

A Cue From Our Crew

Middle-schoolers and high-schoolers are great "extras." Their willing hands and additional energy made every task easier. They moved props, blew up balloons, filled water tables for Preschool Bible Playhouse, and performed a number of miscellaneous tasks. Our crew would highly recommend you recruit a supporting cast of teenagers to use as "production assistants."

Form" (p. 154), or purchase HolyWord Studios registration cards (available from Group Publishing and your local Christian bookstore). Insert copies in your church bulletins, distribute copies in Sunday school classes, and keep a supply in your church office. Encourage parents from your church to preregister their children and their children's friends. This will make your first day more manageable.

☆ **Hold the scheduled leader training meeting.** Plan to meet in a large room where you'll be able to try out some HolyWord Studios snacks and activities. Before the meeting, set up a TV and VCR, and decorate the room using the suggestions provided in the leader training outline (p. 108). Bring the Location Leader manuals and photocopies of the "For Film Crew Leaders Only" handouts (pp. 118-123). Don't forget to provide yummy Movie Munchies for your cast!

☆ **Meet with each Location Leader.** It's a good idea to touch base with each Location Leader on a one-to-one basis. Take each person to lunch, out for ice cream, or simply go for a walk together as you discuss what supplies the leaders need, what concerns they may have, or any aspects of the program they're not clear on. Not only will this prevent miscommunication, but it will help your volunteers know how much you appreciate them!

HolyWord HiNtS

It's a good idea to line up a few extra Film Crew Leaders who will be available in case you have lots of walk-in registrants. Be sure these Film Crew Leaders arrive early on Day 1 so they can step in if necessary. (Because no preparation is needed for Film Crew Leaders, it's easy for people to step in at any point.)

☆ **Provide HolyWord Studios information to your church office.** Fill in your church's information on the community flier on page 134, and photocopy a stack of completed fliers on brightly colored paper to put in your church office. Someone in the office can refer to the fliers if people call with questions about your program and can distribute fliers to people who stop by the office.

If your church has a phone answering machine, you may also want to include HolyWord Studios information in your recorded message. If your church has its own Web site, be sure to add HolyWord Studios information there, too.

A Cue From Our Crew

In preparing for our initial brainstorming time, we purchased snacks such as Junior Mints, popcorn, Good & Plenty, and Hot Tamales. Upon seeing the stack of goodies, the cashier at the grocery store asked, "Are you going to the movies or something?" These treats really do convey your theme!

Two Weeks Before HolyWord Studios

☆ **Check your registration count.** Make sure you have enough Student Books and sticker sheets for each child to have one. Order extras just in case; many churches experience last-minute add-ons, first-day surprises, and unexpected increases as kids bring their friends throughout the week. Also double-check that you have enough Film Crew Leaders, assigning one crew leader to five children.

☆ **Check your supply collection.** Make a final announcement or put a final supply list in your church bulletin. Gather or purchase additional supplies as necessary.

☆ **Continue publicity.** Photocopy and fill out the news release (p. 133), and send copies to your local newspapers, radio stations, and TV stations. Use the snazzy clip art found on the *Sing & Play Soundtrack Music & Clip Art CD* to create fliers, bulletins, posters, and more! This CD contains the thirteen upbeat Sing & Play Soundtrack songs and works with Macintosh and PC-compatible computers.

Announce HolyWord Studios in worship services and other church gatherings. Put bulletin inserts (p. 131) in your church's worship bulletins.

As church members enter your facility, distribute theme-oriented snacks such as Junior Mints, popcorn, Good & Plenty, or Hot Tamales.

Before your worship service, have a few volunteers perform the publicity skit on page 135. Show the promotional segment of the *Sneak Preview* video again.

Mail additional HolyWord Studios invitation postcards as necessary.

☆ **Make backup and emergency plans.** What if it rains during your program? Plan in advance how you'll handle bad weather. You may also want to line up backup Film Crew Leaders in case some drop out.

Inform Location Leaders and Film Crew Leaders of procedures you'll follow if there's a fire or other emergency.

A Cue From Our Crew

Our Location Leaders needed a way to quickly identify the Film Crew Leaders in each group. We provided HolyWord Studios caps for the crew leaders to wear during the week. Crew leaders used metallic paint pens to write their names on their caps, and they even wrote the names of their Film Crew members on the caps. The caps became fun souvenirs for crew leaders to take home at the end of the week. HolyWord Studios caps are available from Group Publishing and your local Christian bookstore.

One Week Before HolyWord Studios

☆ **Dedicate HolyWord Studios staff.** Introduce Location Leaders, Film Crew Leaders, and other volunteers during your church service. Then have your pastor or other church members pray that God will use these workers to touch kids' lives with his love during HolyWord Studios.

☆ **Assign kids to Film Crews.** Photocopy the "Film Crew Roster" (p. 152). You'll need one roster for each Film Crew. Using the preregistration forms you've received, assign children to elementary and preschool Film Crews. Each Film Crew should have no more than five children and one adult or teenage Film Crew Leader. Be sure that each preschool Film Crew has a mix of three-, four-, and five-year-olds.

Here are some additional guidelines for assigning crews:

- ✔ Fill in the "Film Crew Roster" (p. 152) in pencil—you'll probably make changes as you work.
- ✔ Whenever possible, place a child from each age level in each Film Crew. If the age distribution at your program is uneven, include as wide an age range as you can. Avoid forming single-age Film Crews.
- ✔ If a child is bringing a friend, assign the two children to the same Film Crew if possible. If a child is bringing several friends, assign pairs of kids to different Film Crews.
- ✔ In general, it works best to assign siblings to different Film Crews. However, you know the children in your church. Use your judgment as to whether siblings

A Cue From Our Crew

We've received countless letters from Group VBS customers who've admitted they were skeptical about forming combined-age crews. But when these customers took a leap of faith and tried combined-age crews, they were amazed at how well they worked! Most people noted a decline in discipline problems, an increase in cooperation, and a special bonding among crew members.

HolyWord HiNtS

If you're planning for a family VBS, assign entire families to each Film Crew. Then, add single adults, grandparents, visiting children, or smaller families to the crews. Remember to leave several Film Crews open, so you can add new members on opening day!

should be together.

- ✔ If you anticipate behavior problems with certain children or have children with special needs, assign them to Film Crews that have more experienced adult Film Crew Leaders.
- ✔ If you have children who are particularly helpful or cooperative, assign them to Film Crews that have teenage Film Crew Leaders.
- ✔ If you want your program to have a strong outreach emphasis, limit each Film Crew to three or four children. Then encourage kids to fill their crews by bringing their friends!
- ✔ Remember to leave open spaces in a few crews for kids who haven't preregistered.
- ✔ After you've assigned elementary children to Film Crews, assign each crew to one of four larger groups. (Remember, one-fourth of the kids at VBS travel together at a time.) Label these four groups A, B, C, and D—or use your creativity to name them something that fits the movie studio theme, such as Super Stars or Awesome Actors. Film Crews travel with their larger groups as they visit the Locations each day. For more information about assigning Film Crews to groups, see page 142.
- ✔ Once you've finished assigning crews, double-check that you haven't forgotten anyone or double-booked anyone.

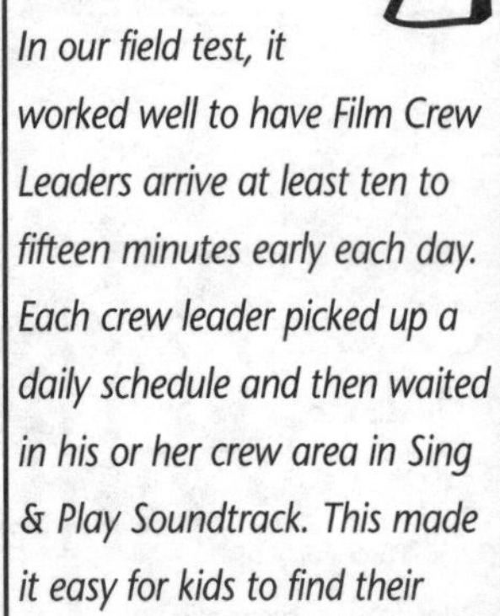

A Cue From Our Crew

In our field test, it worked well to have Film Crew Leaders arrive at least ten to fifteen minutes early each day. Each crew leader picked up a daily schedule and then waited in his or her crew area in Sing & Play Soundtrack. This made it easy for kids to find their crew leaders and settle in right away.

☆ **Meet with Location Leaders again.** Check with each leader to make sure he or she has all the required supplies, and answer any questions he or she may have. Work together to smooth out any last-minute details.

☆ **Decide when and where Location Leaders and Film Crew Leaders will meet at HolyWord Studios each day.** It's a good idea to have your staff arrive early on Day 1 to greet children and assist with registration. Be sure each Film Crew Leader has a large sign with his or her crew number written on it.

☆ **Help Location Leaders decorate their rooms.** Use the decorating ideas found in the catalog, leader manuals, or the general decorating suggestions in the "Facilities: Turn Your Church Into a Blockbuster Bible-Times Movie Set" section of this manual (pp. 58-61) to create a Bible-times movie set atmosphere.

During HolyWord Studios

☆ **Meet with Film Crew Leaders during Sing & Play Soundtrack.** Each day the Sing & Play Soundtrack Leader will excuse Film Crew Leaders for a quick huddle and prayer with you outside the Sing & Play Soundtrack area. This is a great time to ask crew leaders if they have any needs or concerns, make last-minute announcements or schedule changes, and encourage your crew leaders. Lead a prayer, asking God to bless your day, protect everyone, and give all leaders wisdom as they work with each child.

☆ **Register new children.** Make sure you have plenty of workers on hand to register kids the first day! (This is an excellent way to use volunteers who aren't available to help the entire week.) Set up separate registration sites for preregistration check-in and walk-in registration. Follow the Day 1 registration procedures outlined on pages 145-150.

After Day 1, maintain a registration table to register kids who join your program midweek.

☆ **Meet with Location Leaders and Film Crew Leaders after each day's program.** Check in with all HolyWord Studios staff to see what went smoothly and what could be improved for future days. Be prepared to change schedules, rooms, or procedures! You may even need to reassign some Film Crews. Work together to make any necessary changes to ensure that everything runs smoothly.

☆ **Give announcements during Sing & Play Soundtrack or Show Time.** During the course of the program, you may need to change schedules, locations, or Film Crew assignments. You also may have personal messages or lost-and-found items to deliver to participants. Each day, check with the Sing & Play Soundtrack Leader and Show Time Leader to schedule any announcements you'd like everyone to hear.

☆ **Attend Sing & Play Soundtrack and Show Time each day.** These opening and closing activities will give you a good indication of how your program is proceeding. They also provide opportunities for children to see you and to identify you as the Studio Director. On Day 1, you'll announce Film Crew group assignments (A, B, C, D) and will join other staff members in teaching children the motions to "God's Story." Each day, the Sing & Play Soundtrack Leader may call on you to pray before dismissing kids to their Locations. Besides, you'll have fun!

☆ **Make sure all Location Leaders and Film Crew Leaders are present each day.** Arrange for substitutes if necessary. If you're in a pinch for Film Crew Leaders, ask the Sing & Play Soundtrack Leader and Show Time Leader to fill in—or appoint yourself crew leader for a day.

☆ **Make sure Location Leaders and Film Crew Leaders have the supplies they need each day.** Have a runner available to collect or purchase additional supplies if necessary.

☆ **Help with discipline problems as necessary.** In HolyWord Studios field tests (and from real programs across the country!), workers encountered virtually no discipline problems. Each day was so full of fun Bible-learning activities that kids didn't have time to misbehave. Combined-age Film Crews encourage kids to work together instead of squabble, and minor problems can be handled by Location Leaders or Film Crew Leaders.

A Cue From Our Crew

During our field test, we met each afternoon for prayer and lunch and to talk about the highlights of the day. This was a fun time for volunteers to relax and share stories about what had happened during their Locations or about what the kids in their Film Crews had done. Not only did we glean important information (to include in the finished program), but it gave everyone a peek at the other exciting things going on at HolyWord Studios.

HolyWord **HINTS**

It's important to check your registration forms for any mention of food allergies. Let the Movie Munchies Leader know as soon as possible so he or she can make alternative snacks if necessary.

☆ **Stock and maintain a first-aid site.** Keep a good supply of adhesive bandages and first-aid ointment on hand along with phone numbers for local clinics and hospitals. You may also want to keep photocopies of kids' registration forms near your first-aid site. You can use the forms to check for allergies or other health concerns.

☆ **Prepare HolyWord Studios completion certificates for your "stars."** Photocopy and fill out a "And the Winner Is..." certificate (p. 181) for each child. A HolyWord Studios completion certificate is also in the Starter Kit, and additional certificates are available from Group Publishing and your local Christian bookstore.

A Cue From Our Crew

The church that hosts our field test decided to sell the Sing & Play Soundtrack *audiocassettes, then use the proceeds to offset their decorating and supply costs. (They quickly sold out and had to start a waiting list!) Not only did children take home the VBS music they were wild about, but the extra dollars helped the church budget. Everyone benefits!*

☆ **Send the memories home!** We've heard it again and again: "My kids can't stop singing those songs!" Well, when those songs include lyrics such as "We believe in God, and we all need Jesus," "Trust in the Lord with all your heart," or "God is good, all the time," why would you want kids to stop singing them? Plan to provide (or sell) *Sing & Play Soundtrack* audiocassettes or CDs for the kids at your program. Set up a table, complete with information, outside your Show Time area. Check out the reduced prices on page 11 of the HolyWord Studios catalog found in the starter kit.

After HolyWord Studios

☆ **Collect reusable leftover supplies.** Store the supplies in your church's supply closet or resource room for use in future VBS programs or other children's ministry events. If you borrowed supplies such as buckets, laundry baskets, or cassette players, return them to their owners.

☆ **Send your Operation Kid-to-Kid Care Kits to the Kid-to-Kid Send-Off Center.** Take the dollar bills from each bag, then write a check for the total amount. (Make checks payable to "Operation Mobilization.") Place the Care Kits in a large, sturdy box. Be sure to stuff crumpled newspaper or newsprint in any open areas so the box is packed tightly, and enclose your check. Tape the box shut, and then simply affix the mailing label from the Operation Kid-to-Kid brochure in the Starter Kit. Add your church address and the number of kits you're including in the package. Operation Mobilization will distribute your Care Kits around the world! (For more information, see the "Operation Kid-to-Kid" section on pages 33-42.)

HolyWord **HINTS**

Networking is the way to go! If members of another local church are going to hold HolyWord Studios, let them know when you'll be taking down your decorations. Most likely, they'll be glad to help—in exchange for any decorations that you're willing to part with! It's a great way to work together, help each other, and build community spirit.

☆ **Leave rooms decorated for your next church service.** If outreach was an emphasis during HolyWord Studios, you'll be pleased when visitors from your VBS program come for church. They'll feel more comfortable returning to a familiar environment. Also, church members will enjoy getting a glimpse of HolyWord Studios.

☆ **Follow up with HolyWord Studios visitors.** Mail HolyWord Studios follow-up postcards (available from Group Publishing and your local Christian bookstore). Encourage Film Crew Leaders to make personal contact with the members of their Film

Crews within two weeks after HolyWord Studios. Use the additional follow-up ideas on pages 178-179 in this manual.

☆ **Report on your program.** During your next worship service, invite Location Leaders, Film Crew Leaders, and kids who attended HolyWord Studios to share their favorite VBS experiences. If you had a real "Film Crew" make a video during the week, this is the perfect time for its grand premiere! Encourage kids to display their Prop Shop Crafts creations. You may even want to invite the Sing & Play Soundtrack Leader to lead everyone in singing one or two favorite HolyWord Studios songs. Consider hosting a brief "HolyWord Academy Awards" show, at which you present silly awards for "Best Actress in a Bible Skit," "Biggest Appetite at Movie Munchies," or "Best Film Crew Cheer." (When others see how much fun VBS can be, your recruiting will be a breeze next year!)

☆ **Present a slide show or post photos from your program.** Kids (and their parents) love seeing themselves on the "big screen." And colorful photos will bring back memories of a terrific time at HolyWord Studios. Set the whole production to music for an even greater effect.

☆ **Meet with your entire HolyWord Studios staff to evaluate your program.** Celebrate a successful production! Make written notes of good ideas that could be used for next year's program. Note any problems that came up and how they were solved. Brainstorm about ways to avoid similar problems in the future. Include notes of how you adapted the HolyWord Studios materials to fit your church. Record the names of Film Crew Leaders and Location Leaders who are interested in helping again next year. Post the "Encore! A Repeat Performance!" handout (p. 183) and allow interested volunteers sign up for next year's program. (You'll be surprised at the number that will!) Bring the HolyWord Studios evaluation forms included in this manual (pp. 185-186), and have staff members fill them out.

☆ **Thank your staff members for all their hard work.** Photocopy and fill out an "And the Winner Is..." certificate (p. 180) for each Location Leader, Film Crew Leader, and other volunteers. Or use the HolyWord Studios thank you cards and certificates available from Group Publishing and your local Christian bookstore. You could even hand out balloons, flowers, or baked goodies to show your appreciation. For more thematic ideas, see page 179 in the "It's a Wrap!" section.

☆ **Fill out the "HolyWord Studios Evaluation."** Tear out this evaluation form (p. 187), and fill it out completely. Send your completed form to Group Publishing—no postage is necessary! You may also want to give a copy of the form to your church pastor, Christian education director, children's minister, or VBS committee. This helps us plan for the future!

A Cue From Our Crew

You'll notice that this program doesn't include a closing musical, play, or presentation for children to perform. That's because we believe the purpose of VBS is for children to enjoy and experience God's love—not to perform. *Through our field tests, we've watched kids sing praise songs just for the pure joy of singing and worship. We've seen them excitedly experience Bible stories just because God's Word is exciting! When kids are forced to practice songs, memorize lines, or perform for adults, the focus shifts from kids to parents. We encourage you to invite parents to each day's Show Time to give them a view of the Bible truths children are discovering! (If you decide to do a "program," skits and songs are easily adapted from the Sing & Play Soundtrack Leader Manual.)*

A Cue From Our Crew

Recruiting volunteers has never been easier! Our field test church averages at least a 50 percent volunteer return rate. When we asked churches across North America, the numbers went up to 74 percent!

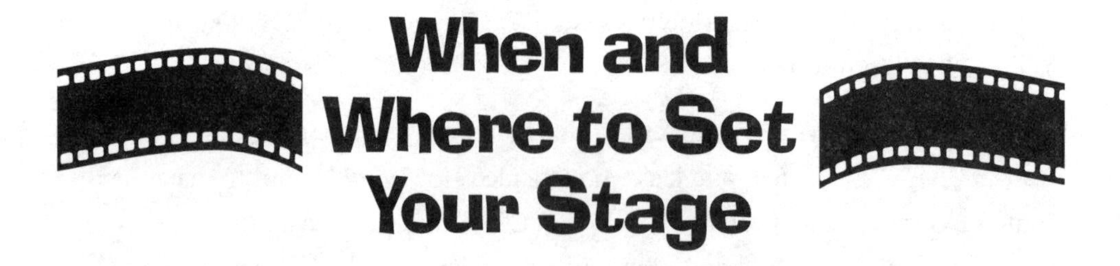

When and Where to Set Your Stage

If your church has put on VBS programs before, you probably have a good idea of the times and settings that work best in your situation. Group's HolyWord Studios works in just about any setting—midweek clubs, day camps, and traditional five-day settings, for example. Use the suggested times and settings listed below to spark creativity as you plan your HolyWord Studios program.

Options for HolyWord Studios Locations

• **Your church:** Many VBS programs are held in local churches. With this approach, you control the facilities, you have many rooms available, and the location is familiar to church members. Plus visitors who come to HolyWord Studios actually visit your church site. (If your church facility isn't large enough, consider teaming up with another local church that might have more room. You'll double your resources and have twice the impact, while showing kids that God's family can do great things when we work together!)

• **A local park:** Kids love being outdoors, and parks draw children who would not normally attend a VBS program. Check with your local parks and recreation department to see about reserving a park or campground for your HolyWord Studios. Church, YMCA, and scout camps provide ideal outdoor settings since they usually have electricity available. Consider renting a large tent or canopy to use in your outdoor setting.

• **Inner city:** Turn your HolyWord Studios program into an inner city outreach opportunity. Invite kids from your church to join inner city kids in an inner city church or neighborhood setting. Even if you use only portions of the HolyWord Studios materials, you'll help needy children and their families understand God's amazing story!

• **A local school:** Since most schools lie dormant for the majority of the summer, consider using their facilities for your program. If public schools are busy with summer classes, check out Christian school facilities in your area.

• **A movie theater:** This is the perfect setting for your HolyWord Studios production! The decorating is done and the theme is set! Many churches rent movie theaters for Sunday morning worship—so why not for a morning VBS? Since most cinemas don't open to the public until afternoon, you'll have the location for several hours.

Options for HolyWord Studios Times

• **Weekday mornings:** Many programs are held for five consecutive weekday mornings. Kids have plenty of energy, and the summer sun isn't quite as hot as in the afternoon. For a change of pace, you could even plan to hold a morning program during your students' spring break!

• **Weekday evenings:** Since many church members work during the day, some churches find it easier to staff an evening program. This could be a special program that you hold for five consecutive days, or it could take the place of an existing midweek program. If you hold your HolyWord Studios program in the evening, you may want to include families. You can offer separate programming for parents and teenagers or include them in HolyWord Studios as full-fledged participants and Film Crew Leaders. Church members of all ages will enjoy visiting the Locations! Each family can form its own Film Crew, or you can mix families and enlist parents as Film Crew Leaders. If you invite families, you'll want to provide child care for children younger than three years old.

• **Midweek clubs:** If your church has a midweek club or another weekly children's program, you may want to use the HolyWord Studios materials for five consecutive weeks. If you use HolyWord Studios during a regularly scheduled midweek program, you'll probably have Location Leaders already in place. Just assign Film Crews and recruit Film Crew Leaders, and you'll be ready to start production!

• **Day camp:** Extend HolyWord Studios to a half-day day camp for kids in your community. (Again, consider holding your day camp during spring break.) We've provided extra crafts, plenty of games, and lots of upbeat songs to keep children actively learning Bible truths...and having a great time!

• **Sunday mornings:** Hold HolyWord Studios during your normal Sunday school or children's church time. This is a great change of pace for summer for both kids and children's workers. (Plus, it's a wonderful way for families to participate!)

• **Weekend retreat:** Invite children or whole families to participate in a weekend retreat held at your church or a local camp. Schedule Day 1 activities for Saturday morning, Days 2 and 3 for Saturday afternoon (after lunch), Day 4 for Saturday evening (after dinner), and Day 5 for Sunday morning.

For a Successful Production...

The following tips will help your evening or intergenerational program go smoothly:

• Start early so young children won't get too tired.

• Consider beginning each session with a simple meal. Recruit a kitchen team to organize potlucks or prepare simple meals such as sandwiches or frozen pizzas. If your church has a lawn or grassy area nearby, you may even want to barbecue. Families will enjoy this casual interaction time, and you'll be able to start your program earlier.

• Make sure children who attend without their families have safe transportation to and from HolyWord Studios. Don't allow children to walk home alone in the dark—even if they live nearby.

• Families come in all shapes and sizes. Be sensitive to single-parent families, childless couples, and children who come alone. You may want to assign family members to separate Film Crews to avoid drawing attention to family differences.

Have fun as you design a production schedule that's best for your HolyWord Studios!

Facilities: Turn Your Church Into a Blockbuster Bible-Times Movie Set

HolyWord HiNtS

VBS Directors continue to amaze us with their creativity, hard work, and incredibly imaginative ideas! If you're a "special effects" expert, who created dazzling sets and ingenious inventions, we'd love to see how you did it! Please send pictures or videocassettes to: VBS Coordinator at Group Publishing, Inc., P.O. Box 481, Loveland, CO 80539. (Sorry, we can't return them!) Or post your photos on our Web site: www.grouppublishing.com. This is a great way to share your ideas with others who may be in the "preproduction" stages!

Atmosphere and environment enhance learning, so decorations are an integral part of HolyWord Studios. They can set the mood for the week and can get children excited about being part of God's amazing story. Following, you'll find a listing of suggested decorations for Locations and other church areas. Remember, these are options and aren't necessary for the success of your HolyWord Studios. If you and others want to go the extra mile, it'll simply enhance the program.

Most decorating items can be found among your church members or can be purchased inexpensively. Have fun! Letting your imagination and creativity go wild, you can create a star-studded environment! Go for it!

Studio Sign-In

Your registration area will be kids' first impression of HolyWord Studios. Think about the entryway of an awards ceremony, where stars are waving, cameras are flashing, and you can feel the excitement. Dress the set with movie posters, lights, and official-looking staff taking (or distributing) tickets.

• **Roll out the red carpet.** These kids are your "stars," and you want them to get a special welcome! Check out thrift stores or carpet stores (for large, but unusable

scraps) for a red carpet that you can roll out for kids to walk on. (Or if you find scraps that aren't red, simply spray paint them!)

• **Create "great light way."** Use white Christmas lights to line your entryway, hallway, or doorway. Chaser lights will make a grand spectacle, making your stars feel truly important!

• **Have costumed staff on hand.** Have volunteers dress up in Bible-times costumes, and/or "techie" clothes to welcome children each day. Your "techies" might carry real or imitation cameras, boom mikes, or wear headphones. (Consider having someone dressed in a blazer, ascot, beret, and dress pants, holding a megaphone, and sitting in a director's chair. Children may have their picture taken with The Director.)

• **Let the fans wave.** Have a few Location Leaders or volunteers act as wild fans, waving autograph books at your stars. These fans can really ham it up with phrases such as, "I've seen every one of your movies!" or "Can I get a picture with you, too?" Kids will eat up the attention, and adults will be assured that their children will be affirmed and loved!

Studio Back Lot

Even your hallways can be eye-catching and exciting! As children travel to their Locations, they'll feel as if they're really on a studio back lot, where you're filming a Bible-times adventure.

• **Create dressing rooms for your "stars."** Place large gold stars on unused doors, along with the words "Private Dressing Room." You may want to have fun with Bible "stars" and add names such as "Moses," "Miriam," or "Pharaoh" to the doors.

• **Let simple signs enhance your environment.** Make simple signs that point the way to studio areas that may not be on your back lot. Include signs directing participants to "Scenery Warehouse," "Costuming," "Sound Stage," or "Special Effects Studio." These simple additions will help kids feel as if they're really on a studio back lot.

• **Photocopy and cut out the arrows from the back of each of the Location**

A Cue From Our Crew

Our field test church got the kids involved even before VBS began! In Sunday school classes, they distributed large sheets of poster board to each child. Kids created their own movie posters (starring themselves), complete with a "celebrity bio" on each poster. During VBS, the posters were hung around the church. The bright posters looked great, were affirming to the kids, and helped everyone get in the action!

Leader Manuals. You'll need at least two arrows per Location to quickly guide children through your facility. Then photocopy, color, and cut out the Location signs from the front of each Location Leader Manual. Hang the posters and arrows so kids can find their way to the correct Locations.

• **Make a "HolyWord Walk of Fame" along one hallway.** Cut large paper stars and tape them to the floor along a hallway. You can add names of Location Leaders, kids, Film Crews, or Bible characters that kids will be learning about during HolyWord Studios. Or allow kids to trace their hand prints and write their autograph inside each star.

• **Let creative costumes decorate for you!** Search local thrift stores for wacky clothes that can be used as costumes. Look for feather boas, wild hats, overcoats, frilly dresses, or robes that double as Bible costumes. When cast members aren't dressing in these silly clothes, drape the costumes on several racks and leave the racks in hallways.

• **Sets can set the stage!** Paint simple Bible-time sets on sheets or large pieces of butcher paper. Consider making the front of a Bible-times house, market, or stable. You say you're not an artist? Simply use the art from the *Sing & Play Soundtrack Music and Clip Art CD.* Run the pictures off on transparencies, then shine the picture on paper or fabric sheets. Trace around the drawings, color them, and you've got an instant backdrop!

Locations

Specific decorating ideas for each Location are listed in the individual leader manuals. Plus, you'll find blockbuster decorating ideas in the catalog in your Starter Kit can! Use the following ideas to reinforce the Bible-time movie sets in all of your Locations.

A Cue From Our Crew

We had a talented artist who designed Bible-times sets on plain sheets. Not only did her artwork add a spectacular splash to our studio, but it allowed her to contribute and participate in a unique way. (Our artist, who had never participated in VBS before, ended up being a Film Crew Leader who excitedly proclaimed, "Wow! I've never seen anything like this before! This is amazing!"

• **Create a "movie scene" in each window.** Use tempera paint to draw perforated film edging around each window, so the scene outdoors becomes a movie scene. This is a fun and easy way to communicate your theme to those inside and out!

• **Hang movie posters.** Creative Bible movie posters (available from Group Publishing or your Christian bookstore) are a fun way to convey your theme...and make kids and adults chuckle along the way. You'll advertise Bible adventures such as "Big," "It's a Wonderful (Eternal) Life," and "Adam's Family." You can keep these up long after VBS, as a fun reminder of the excitement at HolyWord Studios.

• **Let Bible "friends" welcome children at every Location.** Costumed actors will enjoy their roles as guards, camel-traders, priests, or shepherds. They can wait outside the Locations, asking Film Crews what they've been doing. Actors and actresses may hold a "script" (the Bible) and pretend to be memorizing lines or preparing for a big scene. (This is an excellent way to use middle-schoolers and high-schoolers who have a dramatic flair!)

• **Place "sets" everywhere!** This is the time to bring out the Bible-time sets you've used in past VBS programs, Easter pageants, or Christmas programs. Set up Bible-

HolyWord HiNtS
Be sure to have your Film Crew Leaders make poster board or construction paper number signs (in the shape of a star) for each Film Crew. Post each number on a different pew or row of chairs in Sing & Play Soundtrack so Film Crews know where to sit each day.

time tents, canopies, wells, or homes in corners or along walls, then place a "camera" in front of the set. You can make a simple camera by gluing a paper cup to one end of an empty cereal box. Paint the item black and place it on a tripod. Make several cameras and place them throughout your studio.

• **Make it a "light" to remember!** A movie set depends on lights to enhance the scene—so fill your sets with lots of light. Make a simple spotlight by curling a sheet of poster board into a tube (about six- to eight-inches in diameter), then taping it securely. Cover the outside of the tube with aluminum foil. Attach tulle (or thin netting) to the inside of the tube to create a stream of "light," pouring from the light, up to the ceiling or onto the set. Hang each light from the ceiling.

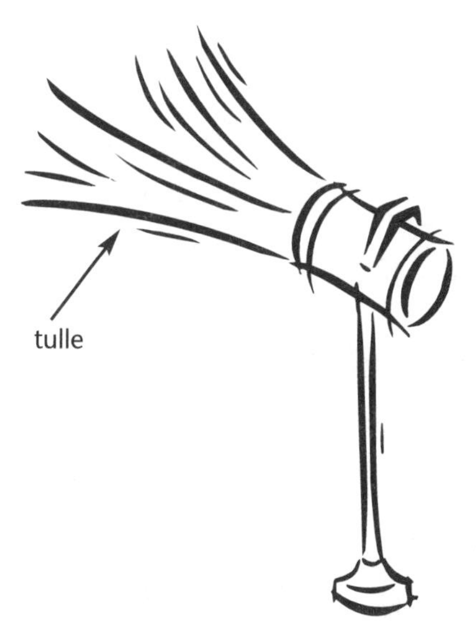

• **Let your imagination run wild!** These ideas are just cues to help you explore the many possibilities. Check out local resources—businesses, libraries, universities, craft and party-supply stores, and video-rental stores—for more ways to turn your facility into HolyWord Studios.

Supplies: Everything You Need for a Five-Star Production

Here are the supplies you'll need for each Location. These supply lists are also printed in their respective leader manuals. Note that some supplies can be shared among Locations.

Sing & Play Soundtrack

- a Bible
- *Sing & Play Soundtrack* audiocassette or CD*
- *Skits & Drama* audiocassette*
- HolyWord Studios sticker sheet*
- a cassette or CD player
- a microphone/sound system
- a hand clapper* or other attention-getting signal
- *Sing & Play Soundtrack Transparencies** (optional)
- an overhead projector (optional)
- a director's slate (optional)

*These items are available from Group Publishing and your local Christian bookstore.

Important Legal Information

For Your Information... When you buy a *Sing & Play Soundtrack* audiocassette, CD, or song lyrics transparencies, you also buy the right to use the thirteen HolyWord Studios songs. You're welcome to play these songs as often as you like. But the companies that own these songs haven't given you (or us!) the right to duplicate any *Sing & Play Soundtrack* products. Making your own copies—even to use at VBS—is against the law...a fact many people don't know. If you do want to have a cassette for every child or leader, we've made bulk buying affordable and easy. Check out the chart in the *Sing & Play Soundtrack Music & Clip Art CD* booklet for more info!

Prop Shop Crafts

You'll need one of the following items for each elementary-age child at HolyWord Studios:

- a TLSeed container and three yards of Star String*
- a baby lima bean
- a large cotton ball
- a Yahoo Yo-Yo and yo-yo string*
- one Incredi-Ball powder packet*
- one snack-size resealable plastic bag
- an Amazing Picture*
- a sheet of HolyWord Studio stickers*

You'll also need the following items:

- cups

HolyWord HINTS

To make your job as easy as possible, we suggest you use HolyWord Studios stickers. Trying to collect a variety of stickers on your own can be time-consuming, frustrating, and expensive. Each sheet of HolyWord Studios stickers contains all the stickers one child will need all week, including job stickers and custom-designed stickers for Prop Shop Crafts and other Locations.

- pitchers of water
- paper towels
- black Sharpie Fine Point markers
- watercolor markers
- pencils
- transparent tape
- construction paper
- Incredi-Ball molds*
- a handful of pushpins
- "Operation Kid-to-Kid" posters*
- a washcloth
- a bath-sized bar of soap
- a four- to six-ounce tube of toothpaste
- a toothbrush
- a comb
- a one-dollar bill (or two Canadian dollars)
- a *Sing & Play Soundtrack* audiocassette or CD* (optional)
- a cassette player (optional)
- a hand clapper* or other attention-getting device

*These items are available from Group Publishing and your local Christian bookstore.

Chadder's Adventure Theater

- a large color TV
- a VCR
- the *Chadder's HolyWord Adventure* video*
- Student Books* (one per child)
- HolyWord Studios sticker sheets* (one sheet per child)
- Bible highlighters* (one per child)
- a hand clapper* or another attention-getting device
- a clock or a watch
- the *Sing & Play Soundtrack* audiocassette or CD* (optional)
- a cassette or CD player (optional)

*These items are available from Group Publishing and your local Christian bookstore.

HolyWord HINTS

When kids arrive for Show Time, they'll probably start talking to their friends in their Film Crews. If there are more than forty kids, you may need more than hand clappers to get their attention. Using a microphone will prevent you from having to shout above kids' voices and will help your voice last all week.

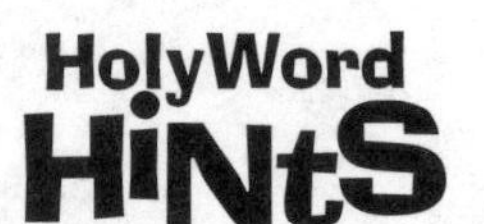

You should be able to find cotton candy at most discount stores (such as KMart or Wal-Mart).

HolyWord HINTS

Check with the Now Playing Games Leader to see if he or she is using a child's wading pool for any games. If so, you may be able to share this supply.

Each day, you'll need

- a Bible,
- a microphone (if there are more than forty kids or if you're using a large room),
- an audiocassette or CD player,
- the *Sing & Play Soundtrack* audiocassette or CD* (from the Sing & Play Soundtrack Leader),
- a clock or a watch, and
- a hand clapper* or another attention-getting device.

You'll also need the following items:

- eight nine-inch balloons,
- cotton candy (enough for each child to have a walnut-sized portion),
- mini hand clappers* (one per child),
- a small table or stand,
- the *Skits & Drama* audiocassette*,
- a large unbreakable bowl containing a packet of red soft drink powder,
- several pitchers filled with water,
- ice cubes (kept in a cooler to keep them from melting),
- a large clear plastic dropcloth (to cover a carpeted floor),
- a child's wading pool,
- an umbrella,
- a raincoat,
- a step stool or chair, and
- star-shaped sunglasses* (one pair per child).
- simple costumes (such as bathrobes, towels, and scarves) for the Israelites who cross the "Red Sea,"
- blue and green balloons (one balloon per child),
- autograph pens,*
- dissolving plastic* cut into small pieces (one piece per child),
- one empty plastic tub,
- one plastic tub filled with warm water,
- a simple costume for the character of Jesus (such as a white sheet and a gold cloth strip to tie around the waist),
- star-shaped mirrors* (one per child),
- a table large enough to hold the Care Kits,
- a doll,
- packing peanuts or cotton balls,
- a large cardboard heart,

• a cross,
• five wrapped gift boxes,
• "Operation Kid-to-Kid" posters from the Prop Shop Crafts Leader, and
• mini bottles of bubbles* (one per child).

*These items are available from Group Publishing and your local Christian bookstore.

Blockbuster Bible Adventures

Things you can find around your home:

• a Bible
• a basket
• bath-tissue tubes (at least six)
• containers for pens (one for each Film Crew)
• paper grocery bags
• lunch-size bags
• newspapers
• empty coffee cans to hold paint (one for each Film Crew)
• a cassette player
• a flashlight
• tunic, sash, sword, and sandals (for Egyptian and Roman soldiers' costumes, as well as for the Israelite scout)
• tunic, sash, jewelry, and sandals (for Pharaoh's daughter's costume)
• aluminum foil
• a fly swatter
• a broom
• strips of white cloth (for Jesus' burial clothes left inside the tomb)
• paper towels
• pinch clothespins
• red powdered drink mix
• a white sheet
• a small lamp
• a belt
• a spray bottle
• a round sofa pillow or piece of cardboard
• a pillowcase

Things you can find around your church:

• self-adhesive notes
• green construction paper

- blue construction paper (if molded produce liners are not available)
- construction paper (various colors)
- marker
- pencils and pens
- scissors
- an X-Acto knife
- a chair (for Pharaoh's throne)
- red washable paint
- paintbrushes (one for each crew)
- a piece of cardboard (to make a cow) or cow stuffed animal
- packing tape
- two plastic pitchers (one empty, one filled with water)
- a clear drinking glass
- large red dot stickers
- plastic forks (two for each child)
- a long table or couch (to hide behind)
- paper plates
- a small table or box

Things you'll need to collect or purchase:

- empty produce boxes with foam liners (to make the Nile River)
- confetti
- paper babies*
- artificial reeds and plants
- 1-foot lengths of wood (one for each crew)
- a roll of newsprint
- cardboard tubes from empty newsprint rolls
- cardboard tubes from empty wrapping paper rolls
- matzo crackers
- sheer blue fabric
- fabric squares
- old tarps or shower curtains
- black plastic
- an olive branch wreath
- balloons
- streamers
- *Skits and Drama* audiocassette*
- a hand clapper* or other attention-getting device

*These items are available from Group Publishing and your local Christian bookstore.

Movie Munchies

FOOD SUPPLIES

Day	Item	Required Amount	Total Number of Participants	Total Required Amount
DAY 1	small flour tortillas	½ per participant	X ____	= ____
	round lunch meat	½ slice per participant	X ____	= ____
	string cheese	½ stick per participant	X ____	= ____
	round cheese crackers	3 per participant	X ____	= ____
	ranch dressing	1-2 teaspoons per participant	X ____	= ____
	paper cupcake liners	1 per participant	X ____	= ____
	drinks	2 quarts for every 10 participants	# of participants ÷ 10= ___	X 2 = ___ qts.
DAY 2	oval crackers	6 per participant	X ____	= ____
	cheese spread or topping	1 tablespoon per participant	X ____	= ____
	small pretzel sticks	9 per participant	X ____	= ____
	red punch	2 quarts for every 10 participants	# of participants ÷ 10= ___	X 2 = ___ qts.
DAY 3	bananas	½ per participant	X ____	= ____
	dessert topping	⅓ cup per participant	X ____	= ____
	blue food coloring	1 vial for every 4 containers of dessert topping	X ____	= ____
	chocolate chips	1 tablespoon per participant	X ____	= ____
	juice or water	2 quarts for every 10 participants	# of participants ÷ 10= ___	X 2 = ___ qts.
DAY 4	plain doughnuts	1 per participant	X ____	= ____
	ready-made frosting	2 tablespoons per participant	X ____	= ____
	food coloring	vials of several colors	X ____	= ____
	sprinkles	1 teaspoon per participant	X ____	= ____
	fat red licorice	3- to 4-inch section per participant	X ____	= ____
	water	2 quarts for every 10 participants	# of participants ÷ 10= ___	X 2 = ___ qts.
DAY 5	cupcakes baked in cupcake liners	1 per participant	X ____	= ____
	ready-made frosting or dessert topping	2 tablespoons per participant	X ____	= ____
	food coloring	vials of several colors	X ____	= ____
	sprinkles	1 teaspoon per participant	X ____	= ____
	fat red licorice	3-inch section per participant	X ____	= ____
	water	2 quarts for every 10 participants	# of participants ÷ 10= ___	X 2 = ___ qts.

A Cue From Our Crew

You might be tempted to purchase shaved lunch meat for today's treat because it's cheaper. But we recommend that you buy round lunch meat and cut it in half. To minimize costs, we used shaved ham but discovered that the preschoolers tended to put it on the tortillas in wads rather than laid out like a "baby blanket." Placing one-half slice of round meat on the tortillas will be easier for small hands.

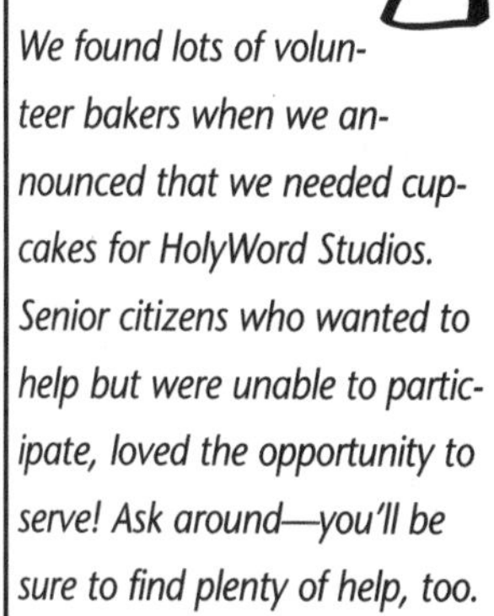

A Cue From Our Crew

We found lots of volunteer bakers when we announced that we needed cupcakes for HolyWord Studios. Senior citizens who wanted to help but were unable to participate, loved the opportunity to serve! Ask around—you'll be sure to find plenty of help, too.

Serving Supplies

Item	Required Amount	Total Number of Participants	Total Required Amount
paper plates	3 per participant	X______________	= ______________
paper cups	5 per participant	X______________	= ______________
napkins	5 per participant	X______________	= ______________
snackmaker (plastic food-handler) gloves	1 pair per participant	X______________	= ______________
pitchers	2 for every 10 participants	X______________	= ______________

Movie Munchies Service Crew Supplies

Item	Required Amount	Total Number of Participants	Total Required Amount
resealable plastic bags (sandwich size)	8 per Movie Munchies Service Crew	X______________	= ______________
resealable plastic bags (quart size)	1 per Movie Munchies Service Crew	X______________	= ______________
paring knives	1 per Movie Munchies Service Crew	X______________	= ______________
butter knives	1 per Movie Munchies Service Crew	X______________	= ______________
plastic knives	2 per Movie Munchies Service Crew	X______________	= ______________

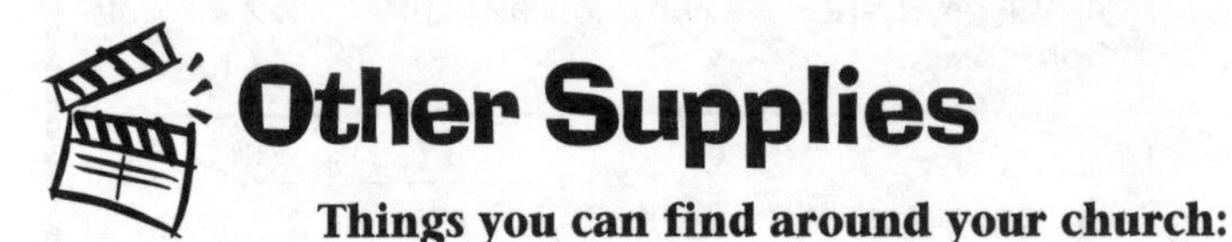

Other Supplies

Things you can find around your church:

- antibacterial soap or individually wrapped hand-wipes
- two or three rolls of paper towels
- scissors
- an assortment of serving bowls, plates, trays, and utensils
- trash cans or trash bags

Things you'll need to collect or purchase:

- *Sing & Play Soundtrack* audiocassette (optional)*
- a chef's hat (optional)*
- a hand clapper* or other attention-getting signal

*These items are available from Group Publishing and your local Christian bookstore.

Now Playing Games

Things you can find around your home:

- a Bible
- rope
- socks (mismatched ones work just fine)
- paper towels
- blindfolds
- plastic cups (2 for each crew)
- plastic spoons (1 for each child)
- bread (1 piece for every child)
- cornstarch

Things you can find around your church:

- a plastic trash can
- markers
- a sprinkler
- a hose and faucet
- a ladder
- strips of fabric
- yarn
- scissors
- a hole punch
- paper clips
- masking tape
- a streamer
- paper

Things you'll need to collect or purchase:

- bedsheets (1 for every 5 to 10 kids)
- a hand clapper* or another attention-getting device
- a roll of newsprint
- magnets
- water balloons
- sturdy laundry baskets (1 for each crew)
- cardboard
- Silly String
- a container of bubbles and a bubble wand
- balloons
- nylon-hose legs (1 for each child)

HolyWord HiNtS

Be sure to check with your Now Playing Games Leader to see which game options he or she has chosen. You may not need all of these supplies.

A Cue From Our Crew

We didn't have time to ask people to donate bedsheets, so we checked out the selection at secondhand stores. There we found twin-bed sheets for about a dollar apiece. Since we didn't have to return them, we were able to tear them up and use the strips for blindfolds later in the week.

A Cue From Our Crew

The cost of Silly String adds up, but if you have room to splurge on any of the games, pick this one. It's definitely worth the cost. Kids loved this game in the field test, and they really got the Point. (You might ask church members to donate this item.)

A Cue From Our Crew

We were absolutely amazed at how the Yuck! grew when it was left in water overnight. A few small packets of Yuck! can easily fill a wading pool.

- wading pools (1 for every 10 kids)
- Yuck!*
- non-toxic ink pads (1 for each crew)
- disposable wipes

*These items are available from Group Publishing and your local Christian bookstore.

Preschool Bible Playhouse

Each day, you'll need

- a Bible
- *Preschool Bible Playhouse* audiocassette*
- a cassette player
- masking tape
- paper
- crayons
- markers
- scissors
- glue sticks
- white glue
- paper towels
- moistened towelettes
- hand clapper* or another attention-getting signal

Things you can find around your home:

- child's wading pool
- flat, white sheet (twin size)
- small people figures (such as Lego or Fisher-Price people)
- small backpacks (2)
- comforters or blankets
- communication devices (such as telephones, walkie-talkies, or megaphones)
- scraps of yarn, fabric, and lace (you'll need brown, green, blue, white, and orange)
- a walking stick or cane
- laundry baskets
- a small wicker basket
- costume jewelry
- hot pads or oven mitts
- winter clothes (such as mittens, scarves, hats, and coats)
- dried peas
- uncooked rice

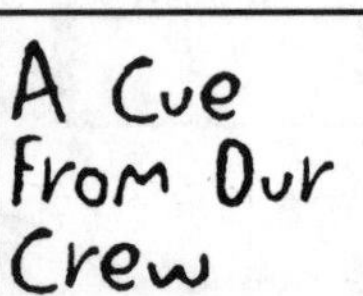

We found flat, white sheets to be very inexpensive at thrift stores. If you can't find them at a thrift store, ask if church members have extras they would be willing to donate.

Things you can find around your church:
- water table or small wading pool
- tables
- overhead projector
- large blocks
- dress-up clothes
- Bible costumes
- stuffed animals
- play dishes
- blue construction paper
- index cards
- balls and other outdoor play equipment
- modeling dough
- paper fasteners

HolyWord HiNtS

Be sure to check with your Preschool Bible Playhouse Director ahead of time to see which Location Stations and Playhouse Playtime activities he or she is planning to do. You may not need all of these supplies.

Things you'll need to collect or purchase:
- HolyWord Studios name badges*
- HolyWord Studios sticker sheets: Preschool*
- Preschool Student Books*
- Film Crew Bags*
- TLSeed Necklace containers and Star String*
- Cool Caps*
- Magnificent Megaphones*
- All-Star Frames and puffy stars*
- cotton balls
- rye grass seed
- crepe paper streamers
- feathers
- craft sticks
- plastic frogs and grasshoppers
- PVC piping and joints
- adhesive Velcro
- poster board
- rope
- wood
- nails
- string
- eyelet screws

*These items are available from Group Publishing and your local Christian bookstore.

This great tip comes from churches that have fine-tuned the art of collecting VBS supplies! It just doesn't get any easier!

1. Photocopy the "We're Collecting Props" ticket below on colored paper. Designate a different color paper for each Location—for example, blue paper for Prop Shop Crafts, orange paper for Movie Munchies, and green paper for Preschool Bible Playhouse.

2. Fill in the information on each ticket. Indicate whether the item needs to be donated (items that will be used up, such as food) or borrowed (items that can be returned, such as sheets or inflatable tubes).

3. Cut apart the tickets, and post them on a bulletin board in a high-traffic area of your church. Make an announcement to inform church members that this is a simple way to help with HolyWord Studios.

4. As items are delivered to the specified area, sort them by the color of the attached ticket. Just before HolyWord Studios begins, collect the tickets and sort them into donated and borrowed items.

5. After VBS, simply have Location Leaders retrieve the borrowed items. Match the items with their tickets, and return the items to their owners.

We're Collecting Props

Item Needed: ______________________________

Donated Borrowed

HolyWord Studios Director: ______________________________

Phone: ______________________________

Your Name: ______________________________

Phone: ______________________________

Please return this item to me by ______________________________

Please attach this ticket to the item and deliver it to ______________________________

by ______________________________(date). Thank you.

Daily Supplies

Many VBS Directors requested a daily supply list, so they could see what days certain supplies were needed. Check out the chart below to see if there are supplies that can be shared between Locations. Movie Munchies is not included in the chart, due to

LOCATION	SUPPLIES YOU'LL USE EVERY DAY...	DAY 1	DAY 2
SING & PLAY SOUNDTRACK	A Bible, *Sing & Play Soundtrack* audiocassette or CD*, *Skits & Drama* audiocassette*, HolyWord Studios sticker sheet*, a cassette or CD player, photocopies of the "Who's Who on the Crew?" handout, a microphone/sound system, a hand clapper*, *Sing & Play Soundtrack Transparencies** (optional), an overhead projector (optional), a director's slate (optional)		
PROP SHOP CRAFTS	*Sing & Play Soundtrack* audiocassette or CD* (optional), cassette player (optional), paper towels, "Operation Kid-to-Kid" posters*, hand clapper* or other attention-getting device	TLSeed containers and Star String*, baby lima beans, large cotton balls, cups of water, HolyWord Studio stickers*, black Sharpie Fine Point markers	Yahoo Yo-Yos and yo-yo string*, watercolor markers, pushpins, pencils, a washcloth, a bath-sized bar of soap, a four- to six-ounce tube of toothpaste, a toothbrush, a comb, a one-dollar bill (or two Canadian dollars), Operation Kid-to-Kid resealable bags*, bandages from a Student Book*, Operation Kid-to-Kid newsletters from Student Books*
BLOCKBUSTER BIBLE ADVENTURES	A Bible	Empty produce boxes; blue construction paper; a couch or long table; green construction paper; bath-tissue tubes (at least six); clear packing tape; scissors; an X-Acto knife; artificial reeds and plants; a basket; tunic, sash, sword, and sandals (for Egyptian soldier); tunic, sash, jewelry, and sandals (for Pharaoh's daughter); paper baby cutouts*; pens; containers for the pens (one for each crew); two copies of "Finding Baby Moses" script; *Skits and Drama* audiocassette*; a cassette player	A clear plastic glass, a spray bottle, red powdered drink mix, two plastic pitchers (one filled with water), a small bag of confetti, pinch clothespins, a cardboard cow or stuffed animal, large red dot stickers, a fly swatter, white paper wads, a pillowcase, a broom, a chair, a box or small table, aluminum foil, empty newsprint rolls, a copy of the "Pharaoh and the Plagues" script, construction paper fish with Xs for eyes
NOW PLAYING GAMES	A hand clapper* or another attention-getting device	Bedsheets (1 for every 5 to 10 kids), a plastic trash can, a roll of newsprint, a blue marker, magnets, water balloons, sturdy laundry baskets (1 for each crew), masking tape	Cardboard (3 pieces for each crew), Silly String (1 can for each crew), photocopies of the "Plague" handout (p. 26 in the Now Playing Games Leader Manual) (1 for every 9 kids), scissors, masking tape, newsprint, markers (1 for each crew), blindfolds (1 for each crew)
CHADDER'S ADVENTURE THEATER	A large color TV, a VCR, *Chadder's HolyWord Adventure* video*, Student Books*, HolyWord Studios sticker sheets*, Bible highlighters*, hand clapper* or another attention-getting device, a clock or a watch, *Sing & Play Soundtrack* audiocassette or CD* (optional), a cassette or CD player (optional)		
SHOW TIME	A Bible, a microphone (if there are more than forty kids or if you're using a large room), an audiocassette or CD player, the *Sing & Play Soundtrack* audiocassette or CD (from the Sing & Play Soundtrack Leader), a clock or a watch, hand clapper or another attention-getting device	Eight nine-inch balloons, cotton candy*, mini hand clappers*	A small table or stand, the *Skits & Drama* audiocassette*, a large unbreakable bowl containing a packet of red soft drink powder, several pitchers filled with water, ice cubes (kept in a cooler to keep them from melting), a large clear plastic dropcloth (to cover a carpeted floor), a child's wading pool, an umbrella, a raincoat, a step stool or chair, star-shaped sunglasses*

*These items are available from Group Publishing and your local Christian bookstore.

the specific nature of the food items. Also, check with the Preschool Director to see what supplies he or she will need each day.

DAY 3	DAY 4	DAY 5
Incredi-Ball powder packets*, Incredi-Ball molds*, cups, small pitchers of water, snack-sized resealable bags, HolyWord Studios sticker sheets*	Amazing Picture frames*, watercolor markers, black Sharpie Fine Point permanent markers, transparent tape	Construction paper, markers or crayons, Care Kit supplies, HolyWord Studio sticker sheets*, Elementary Student Book*
Newspaper, brown paper grocery bags (twelve times the number of crews each session), clear packing tape, old tarps or shower curtains, red washable paint, coffee cans or other paint containers with lids (one per crew), paintbrushes (one per crew), paper plates, matzo crackers, paper towels (both wet and dry) for cleanup, sheer blue material, spray bottle of water, material squares (one for each crew member), one copy of the "Israelite Scout" script, tunic and sandals for the Israelite scout, *Skits and Drama* audiocassette*, a cassette player	A white sheet; a small lamp (without shade); clear packing tape; a belt or length of rope; a cardboard cross (made from empty wrapping paper tubes); a stand for the cross; an olive branch wreath; paper-bag door frames from Day 3; a pillow or piece of cardboard; newsprint; marker; self-adhesive notes; pens; black plastic (to darken room); paper grocery bags; scissors; plastic forks (two per child); 1-foot lengths of wood (one per crew); a flashlight; a tunic, sash, sword, and sandals; foil sheet and armrests from Pharaoh's throne; strips of white cloth	A cassette player, *Skits and Drama* audiocassette*, *Sing & Play Soundtrack* audiocassette: "We Believe in God,"* balloons, tape, streamers, containers of pens (one per film crew)
Balloons; masking tape; two long lengths of rope; a sprinkler; a hose and faucet; a container of bubbles and a bubble wand; a ladder; a Bible; socks; strips of fabric, paper towels, or T-shirts; yarn; scissors; photocopies of the "Whopper" handout (p. 37 in the Now Playing Games Leader Manual); a hole punch	Balloons, panty-hose legs, scissors, paper, masking tape, wading pools, Yuck!*, paper clips or marbles, paper towels, blindfolds, plastic cups, plastic spoons, cornstarch, water	Non-toxic ink pads, photocopies of the "Thumb Prints on Your Hand" handout (p. 48 in the Now Playing Games Leader Manual), disposable wipes, a streamer, bread, paper, masking tape
Simple costumes (such as bathrobes, towels, and scarves) for the Israelites who cross the "Red Sea"; blue and green balloons; autograph pens.*	Dissolving plastic* cut into small pieces, one empty plastic tub, one plastic tub filled with warm water, a simple costume for the character of Jesus (such as a white sheet and a gold cloth strip to tie around the waist), star-shaped mirrors*	A table large enough to hold the Care Kits, a doll, packing peanuts or cotton balls, a large cardboard heart, a cross, five wrapped gift boxes, "Operation Kid-to-Kid" posters from the Prop Shop Crafts Leader, mini bottles of bubbles*

Daily Schedules

> **A Cue From Our Crew**
>
> *We discovered that it's a good idea to arrange your Film Crews so that you have at least one experienced adult crew leader in each lettered group. Adults can offer encouragement, leadership, or helpful advice to younger crew leaders.*

Each day when kids come to HolyWord Studios, they visit seven Locations. All Film Crews visit Sing & Play Soundtrack, Movie Munchies, and Show Time together. In between these activities, the remaining Locations run simultaneously. Location Leaders repeat their activities four times, with a different group of Film Crews each time. When it's time for groups to move to a new Location, walk through HolyWord Studios shake the hand clappers (or use some other attention-getting device). This helps kids, crew leaders, and Location Leaders stay on schedule.

After you've assigned kids to Film Crews, you assign Film Crews to groups. Each group consists of one-fourth of the elementary-age Film Crews at HolyWord Studios. To eliminate confusion with Film Crew numbers, use letters, colors, or creative critters to label these four groups.

For example, if you have sixty kids, you will end up with twelve Film Crews of five kids. You will then assign the crews to larger groups in this way:

A—crews 1-3
B—crews 4-6
C—crews 7-9
D—crews 10-12

If you have 150 kids, you will end up with thirty Film Crews of five kids. You will then assign the crews to larger groups in this way:

A—crews 1-7
B—crews 8-15
C—crews 16-22
D—crews 23-30

If you have more than 150 kids, set up double Locations for Now Playing Games, Blockbuster Bible Adventures, Prop Shop Crafts, and Chadder's Adventure Theater. For more information on running double Locations, see the diagram on page 23.

You'll notice on the "Daily Schedule and Announcements" pages (pp. 76-84) that groups visit the Locations in a different order each day. This schedule shift provides welcome variety for kids and allows a different group to perform Movie Munchies Service each day. Movie Munchies Service is extremely important to the crews, who get a chance to share God's love.

Preschool children will keep the same schedule each day but will perform Movie Munchies Service on Day 1. Preschoolers will leave their room and join older kids for Sing & Play Soundtrack and Show Time. They view each day's *Chadder's HolyWord Adventure* segment while older kids are enjoying Movie Munchies. All other preschool activities take place in or near the Preschool Bible Playhouse room.

Use the sample morning and evening schedules (pp. 78-79) to plan your VBS times. Then fill in the times on the "Daily Schedule and Announcements: Day 1" (p. 80). Note any announcements you want to pass on to your staff, and then photocopy and distribute the schedule. Don't forget to give copies to the Film Crew Leaders! Each day before HolyWord Studios, fill in the appropriate day's schedule with times and announcements.

HolyWord HiNtS

Everyone loves a joke, silly anecdote, or comical quote. Consider adding "smile-inducers" to your daily schedules—it's an easy way to create a smiling staff!

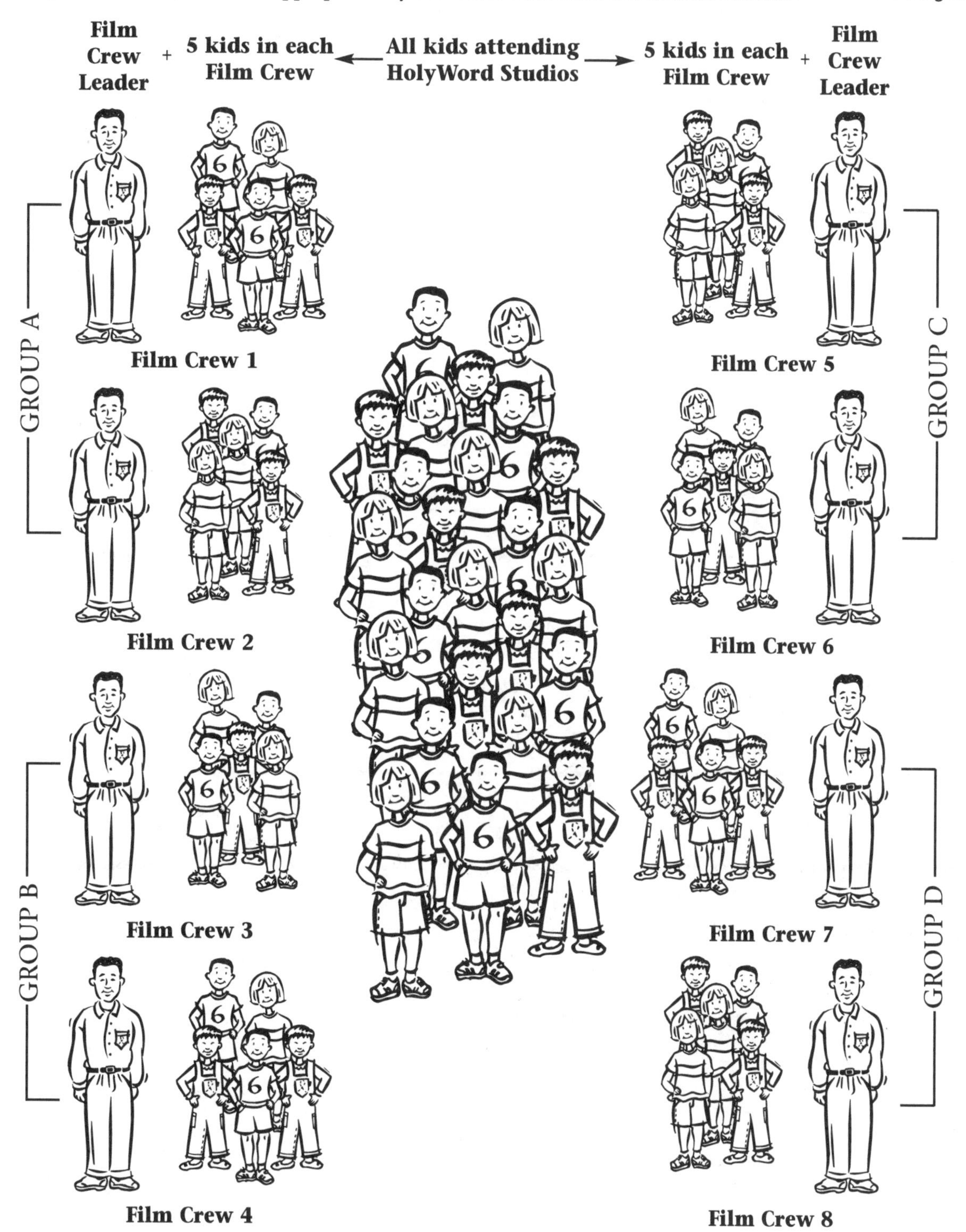

Sample

HolyWord Studios

Morning Schedule (8:30-11:30)

Daily Schedule

Time	Group A Crews 1-5	Group B Crews 6-10	Group C Crews 11-15	Group D Crews 16-20	Preschool
8:30-8:55	Sing & Play Soundtrack	Sing & Play Soundtrack	Sing & Play Soundtrack	Sing & Play Soundtrack	Preschool Bible Playhouse
Allow five minutes to scout your next Location.					
9:00-9:20	Blockbuster Bible Adventures	Prop Shop Crafts	Now Playing Games	Chadder's Adventure Theater	Movie Munchies Service
Allow five minutes to scout your next Location.					
9:25-9:45	Prop Shop Crafts	Now Playing Games	Chadder's Adventure Theater	Blockbuster Bible Adventures	Preschool Bible Playhouse
Allow five minutes to scout your next Location.					
9:50-10:10	Movie Munchies	Movie Munchies	Movie Munchies	Movie Munchies	Chadder's Adventure Theater
Allow five minutes to scout your next Location.					
10:15-10:35	Now Playing Games	Chadder's Adventure Theater	Blockbuster Bible Adventures	Prop Shop Crafts	Preschool Bible Playhouse
Allow five minutes to scout your next Location.					
10:40-11:00	Chadder's Adventure Theater	Blockbuster Bible Adventures	Prop Shop Crafts	Now Playing Games	Preschool Bible Playhouse
Allow five minutes to scout your next Location.					
11:05-11:30	Show Time	Show Time	Show Time	Show Time	Show Time

Sample

HolyWord Studios

Evening Schedule (6:30-9:10)*

Daily Schedule

Time	Group A Crews 1-5	Group B Crews 6-10	Group C Crews 11-15	Group D Crews 16-20	Preschool
6:30-6:45	Sing & Play Soundtrack	Sing & Play Soundtrack	Sing & Play Soundtrack	Sing & Play Soundtrack	Preschool Bible Playhouse
		Allow five minutes to scout your next Location.			
6:50-7:10	Blockbuster Bible Adventures	Prop Shop Crafts	Now Playing Games	Chadder's Adventure Theater	Movie Munchies Service
		Allow five minutes to scout your next Location.			
7:15-7:35	Prop Shop Crafts	Now Playing Games	Chadder's Adventure Theater	Blockbuster Bible Adventures	Preschool Bible Playhouse
		Allow five minutes to scout your next Location.			
7:40-7:55	Movie Munchies	Movie Munchies	Movie Munchies	Movie Munchies	Chadder's Adventure Theater
		Allow five minutes to scout your next Location.			
8:00-8:20	Now Playing Games	Chadder's Adventure Theater	Blockbuster Bible Adventures	Prop Shop Crafts	Preschool Bible Playhouse
		Allow five minutes to scout your next Location.			
8:25-8:45	Chadder's Adventure Theater	Blockbuster Bible Adventures	Prop Shop Crafts	Now Playing Games	Preschool Bible Playhouse
		Allow five minutes to scout your next Location.			
8:50-9:10	Show Time	Show Time	Show Time	Show Time	Show Time

*Kids will need at *least* twenty minutes to complete each Location. If you need to end your program promptly at 9 p.m., shorten your "scouting" time to two or three minutes between each Location.

Daily Schedule and Announcements

God cares for us.

"For your Father knows what you need before you ask him (Matthew 6:8b).

Daily Schedule

Time	Group A Crews_____	Group B Crews_____	Group C Crews_____	Group D Crews_____	Preschool
	Sing & Play Soundtrack	Sing & Play Soundtrack	Sing & Play Soundtrack	Sing & Play Soundtrack	Preschool Bible Playhouse
Allow five minutes to scout your next Location.					
	Blockbuster Bible Adventures	Prop Shop Crafts	Now Playing Games	Chadder's Adventure Theater	Movie Munchies Service
Allow five minutes to scout your next Location.					
	Prop Shop Crafts	Now Playing Games	Chadder's Adventure Theater	Blockbuster Bible Adventures	Preschool Bible Playhouse
Allow five minutes to scout your next Location.					
	Movie Munchies	Movie Munchies	Movie Munchies	Movie Munchies	Chadder's Adventure Theater
Allow five minutes to scout your next Location.					
	Now Playing Games	Chadder's Adventure Theater	Blockbuster Bible Adventures	Prop Shop Crafts	Preschool Bible Playhouse
Allow five minutes to scout your next Location.					
	Chadder's Adventure Theater	Blockbuster Bible Adventures	Prop Shop Crafts	Now Playing Games	Preschool Bible Playhouse
Allow five minutes to scout your next Location.					
	Show Time	Show Time	Show Time	Show Time	Show Time

Today's announcements:

Daily Schedule and Announcements

God protects us.

"Come to me, all you who are weary and burdened, and I will give you rest" (Matthew 11:28).

Daily Schedule

Time	Group A Crews_____	Group B Crews_____	Group C Crews_____	Group D Crews_____	Preschool
	Sing & Play Soundtrack	Sing & Play Soundtrack	Sing & Play Soundtrack	Sing & Play Soundtrack	Sing & Play Soundtrack
Allow five minutes to scout your next Location.					
	Blockbuster Bible Adventures	Prop Shop Crafts	Movie Munchies Service	Chadder's Adventure Theater	Preschool Bible Playhouse
Allow five minutes to scout your next Location.					
	Prop Shop Crafts	Now Playing Games	Chadder's Adventure Theater	Blockbuster Bible Adventures	Preschool Bible Playhouse
Allow five minutes to scout your next Location.					
	Movie Munchies	Movie Munchies	Movie Munchies	Movie Munchies	Chadder's Adventure Theater
Allow five minutes to scout your next Location.					
	Now Playing Games	Chadder's Adventure Theater	Blockbuster Bible Adventures	Prop Shop Crafts	Preschool Bible Playhouse
Allow five minutes to scout your next Location.					
	Chadder's Adventure Theater	Blockbuster Bible Adventures	Prop Shop Crafts	Now Playing Games	Preschool Bible Playhouse
Allow five minutes to scout your next Location.					
	Show Time	Show Time	Show Time	Show Time	Show Time

Today's announcements:

Daily Schedule and Announcements

God loves us.

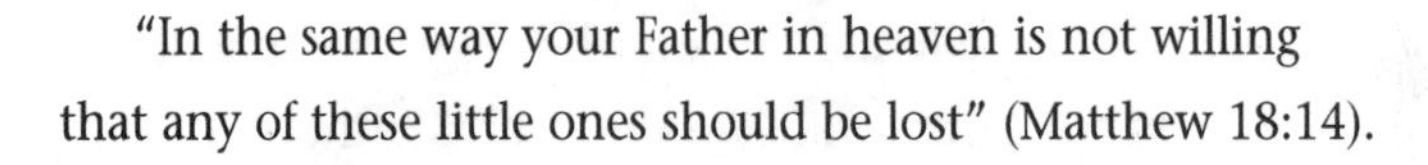

"In the same way your Father in heaven is not willing that any of these little ones should be lost" (Matthew 18:14).

Daily Schedule

Time	Group B Crews_____	Group C Crews_____	Group D Crews_____	Group A Crews_____	Preschool
	Sing & Play Soundtrack	Sing & Play Soundtrack	Sing & Play Soundtrack	Sing & Play Soundtrack	Sing & Play Soundtrack
Allow five minutes to scout your next Location.					
	Blockbuster Bible Adventures	Prop Shop Crafts	Movie Munchies Service	Chadder's Adventure Theater	Preschool Bible Playhouse
Allow five minutes to scout your next Location.					
	Prop Shop Crafts	Now Playing Games	Chadder's Adventure Theater	Blockbuster Bible Adventures	Preschool Bible Playhouse
Allow five minutes to scout your next Location.					
	Movie Munchies	Movie Munchies	Movie Munchies	Movie Munchies	Chadder's Adventure Theater
Allow five minutes to scout your next Location.					
	Now Playing Games	Chadder's Adventure Theater	Blockbuster Bible Adventures	Prop Shop Crafts	Preschool Bible Playhouse
Allow five minutes to scout your next Location.					
	Chadder's Adventure Theater	Blockbuster Bible Adventures	Prop Shop Crafts	Now Playing Games	Preschool Bible Playhouse
Allow five minutes to scout your next Location.					
	Show Time	Show Time	Show Time	Show Time	Show Time

Today's announcements:

Daily Schedule and Announcements

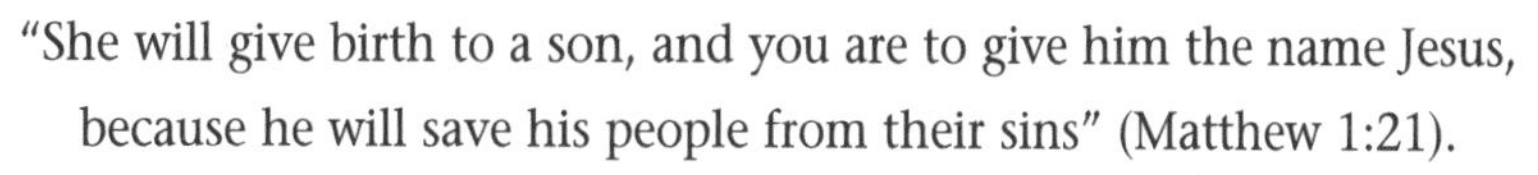

God saves us.

"She will give birth to a son, and you are to give him the name Jesus, because he will save his people from their sins" (Matthew 1:21).

Daily Schedule

Time	Group C Crews______	Group D Crews______	Group A Crews______	Group B Crews______	Preschool
	Sing & Play Soundtrack	Sing & Play Soundtrack	Sing & Play Soundtrack	Sing & Play Soundtrack	Sing & Play Soundtrack
Allow five minutes to scout your next Location.					
	Blockbuster Bible Adventures	Prop Shop Crafts	Movie Munchies Service	Chadder's Adventure Theater	Preschool Bible Playhouse
Allow five minutes to scout your next Location.					
	Prop Shop Crafts	Now Playing Games	Chadder's Adventure Theater	Blockbuster Bible Adventures	Preschool Bible Playhouse
Allow five minutes to scout your next Location.					
	Movie Munchies	Movie Munchies	Movie Munchies	Movie Munchies	Chadder's Adventure Theater
Allow five minutes to scout your next Location.					
	Now Playing Games	Chadder's Adventure Theater	Blockbuster Bible Adventures	Prop Shop Crafts	Preschool Bible Playhouse
Allow five minutes to scout your next Location.					
	Chadder's Adventure Theater	Blockbuster Bible Adventures	Prop Shop Crafts	Now Playing Games	Preschool Bible Playhouse
Allow five minutes to scout your next Location.					
	Show Time	Show Time	Show Time	Show Time	Show Time

Today's announcements:

Daily Schedule and Announcements

God is always with us.

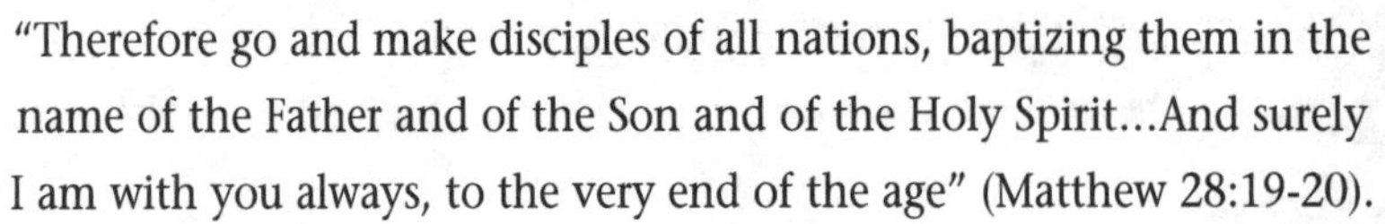

"Therefore go and make disciples of all nations, baptizing them in the name of the Father and of the Son and of the Holy Spirit...And surely I am with you always, to the very end of the age" (Matthew 28:19-20).

Daily Schedule

Time	Group D Crews_____	Group A Crews_____	Group B Crews_____	Group C Crews_____	Preschool
	Sing & Play Soundtrack	Sing & Play Soundtrack	Sing & Play Soundtrack	Sing & Play Soundtrack	Sing & Play Soundtrack
Allow five minutes to scout your next Location.					
	Blockbuster Bible Adventures	Prop Shop Crafts	Movie Munchies Service	Chadder's Adventure Theater	Preschool Bible Playhouse
Allow five minutes to scout your next Location.					
	Prop Shop Crafts	Now Playing Games	Chadder's Adventure Theater	Blockbuster Bible Adventures	Preschool Bible Playhouse
Allow five minutes to scout your next Location.					
	Movie Munchies	Movie Munchies	Movie Munchies	Movie Munchies	Chadder's Adventure Theater
Allow five minutes to scout your next Location.					
	Now Playing Games	Chadder's Adventure Theater	Blockbuster Bible Adventures	Prop Shop Crafts	Preschool Bible Playhouse
Allow five minutes to scout your next Location.					
	Chadder's Adventure Theater	Blockbuster Bible Adventures	Prop Shop Crafts	Now Playing Games	Preschool Bible Playhouse
Allow five minutes to scout your next Location.					
	Show Time	Show Time	Show Time	Show Time	Show Time

Today's announcements:

Recruitment

Bringing in an All-Star Cast

Casting Location Leaders

Location Leaders are the backbone of your HolyWord Studios cast. These are the people who teach and show God's love to the kids who attend your program. Kids look forward to seeing the Location Leaders each day—and so do you! You need at least eight volunteers—one leader for each of the following Locations:

- Sing & Play Soundtrack
- Prop Shop Crafts
- Now Playing Games
- Movie Munchies
- Blockbuster Bible Adventures
- Chadder's Adventure Theater
- Show Time
- Preschool Bible Playhouse

If you're expecting more than 150 elementary-age kids to attend HolyWord Studios, you may want to double up on Location Leaders. Purchase an additional leader manual for each Location, and run two sessions of each Location simultaneously. This will help keep Location group sizes manageable (fewer than thirty kids per session). Or have two Location Leaders team teach a large group of kids in a larger classroom.

Location Leaders should be adults or mature older teenagers. You'll find a specific job description for each Location Leader in the following pages. In general, you should look for Location Leaders who are

- dependable church members or regular attendees,
- enthusiastic about working with children,
- excited about serving at HolyWord Studios,
- patient and kind,
- good communicators,
- comfortable speaking in front of groups of thirty or more, and
- gifted in their Location areas.

Use the details in the following job descriptions to help you enlist leaders for the Locations. Give each leader a copy of his or her job description, and offer to address any questions or concerns that may arise. Invite Location Leaders and Film Crew Leaders to your scheduled leader training.

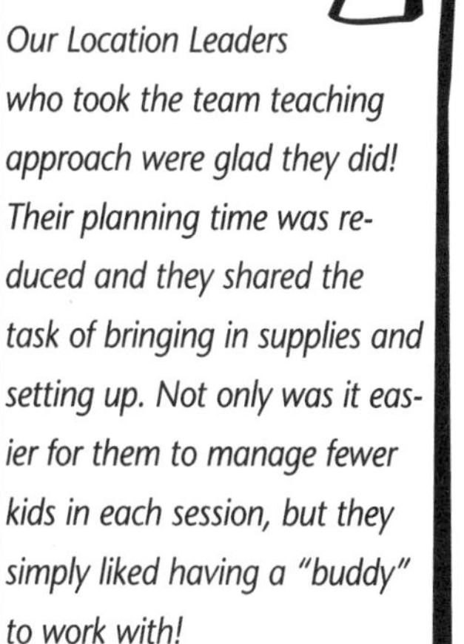

A Cue From Our Crew

Our Location Leaders who took the team teaching approach were glad they did! Their planning time was reduced and they shared the task of bringing in supplies and setting up. Not only was it easier for them to manage fewer kids in each session, but they simply liked having a "buddy" to work with!

HolyWord HINTS

If you want to appoint an Assistant Studio Director, ask the Sing & Play Soundtrack Leader or the Show Time Leader. Because these two leaders present their material only once each day, they'll be free to help you handle last-minute details.

A Cue From Our Crew

Talk about easy recruiting! After our field test, several Location Leaders volunteered to lead their areas next year! Other churches have reported similar results, with a high volunteer return rate.

List the names, addresses, and phone numbers of your Location Leaders in the chart below so you're able to quickly access the information.

Once you've enlisted your Location Leaders, you're ready to begin recruiting Film Crew Leaders!

Casting Location Leaders

Location	Leader's Name	Address	Phone Number	Other Notes
Sing & Play Soundtrack				
Prop Shop Crafts				
Now Playing Games				
Movie Munchies				
Blockbuster Bible Adventures				
Chadder's Adventure Theater				
Show Time				
Preschool Bible Playhouse				

Job Description

Sing & Play Soundtrack Leader

Qualifications

You'll be a successful Sing & Play Soundtrack Leader if you

- ☆ love the Lord and love children,
- ☆ have experience leading songs or singing with children,
- ☆ can motivate and energize kids, and
- ☆ are comfortable speaking in front of large groups.

Responsibilities

As a Sing & Play Soundtrack Leader, you'll be responsible for

- ☆ attending scheduled leader training,
- ☆ repeating the daily Bible Point as you teach,
- ☆ learning the music and motions for thirteen HolyWord Studios songs,
- ☆ teaching kids the words and motions to several songs each day,
- ☆ leading singing for the entire VBS,
- ☆ assisting with Show Time programs each day, and
- ☆ assisting the HolyWord Studios Director as needed.

Related Interests

If you enjoy any of the following activities, you'll enjoy leading Sing & Play Soundtrack:

- ★ playing a musical instrument,
- ★ directing or singing in your church choir,
- ★ leading worship, and
- ★ acting or drama.

Join the cast at HolyWord Studios:
Where kids star in God's story!

Job Description

Prop Shop Crafts Leader

Qualifications

You'll be a successful Prop Shop Crafts Leader if you

- ☆ love the Lord and love children,
- ☆ are creative and fun-loving,
- ☆ can give clear directions to children, and
- ☆ show patience while working with lots of children.

Responsibilities

As a Prop Shop Crafts Leader, you'll be responsible for

- ☆ attending scheduled leader training meetings,
- ☆ collecting necessary supplies,
- ☆ preparing sample crafts before HolyWord Studios,
- ☆ explaining and encouraging children to carry out Operation Kid-to-Kid,
- ☆ repeating the daily Bible Point as you teach,
- ☆ helping children create one-of-a-kind crafts,
- ☆ leading four sessions of Prop Shop Crafts each day, and
- ☆ assisting with Show Time as needed.

Related Interests

If you enjoy any of the following activities, you'll enjoy leading Prop Shop Crafts:

- ★ science projects,
- ★ missions projects,
- ★ arts and crafts, and
- ★ working with your hands.

Join the cast at HolyWord Studios:

Where kids star in God's story!

Now Playing Games Leader

Qualifications

You'll be a successful Now Playing Games Leader if you

- ☆ love the Lord and love children;
- ☆ enjoy playing games;
- ☆ are positive, active, and energetic; and
- ☆ can organize and motivate children.

Responsibilities

As a Now Playing Games Leader, you'll be responsible for

- ☆ attending scheduled leader training,
- ☆ repeating the daily Bible Point as you teach,
- ☆ collecting necessary supplies for Now Playing Games,
- ☆ clearly explaining each game,
- ☆ leading three sessions of Now Playing Games each day,
- ☆ assisting with Movie Munchies Service each day, and
- ☆ assisting with Show Time as needed.

Related Interests

If you enjoy any of the following activities, you'll enjoy leading Now Playing Games:

- ★ team sports,
- ★ outdoor recreational activities, and
- ★ encouraging others to do their best.

Join the cast at HolyWord Studios:

Where kids star in God's story!

Job Description

Movie Munchies Leader

Qualifications

You'll be a successful Movie Munchies Leader if you

- ☆ love the Lord and love children,
- ☆ enjoy cooking and food preparation,
- ☆ believe children can accomplish big tasks,
- ☆ can give clear directions to children, and
- ☆ accept and encourage children's abilities.

Responsibilities

As a Movie Munchies Leader, you'll be responsible for

- ☆ attending scheduled leader training,
- ☆ repeating the daily Bible Point as you teach,
- ☆ coordinating food supplies for each day's snack,
- ☆ setting up assembly lines to help kids prepare each day's snack,
- ☆ serving snacks to the entire HolyWord Studios,
- ☆ cleaning up the Movie Munchies area after snacks are served, and
- ☆ assisting with Show Time as needed.

Related Interests

If you enjoy any of the following activities, you'll enjoy leading Movie Munchies:

- ★ preparing and serving food,
- ★ maintaining a clean environment,
- ★ working in a kitchen or restaurant, and
- ★ organizing and supervising teams of people.

Join the cast at HolyWord Studios:

Where kids star in God's story!

Job Description

Blockbuster Bible Adventures Leader

Qualifications

You'll be a successful Blockbuster Bible Adventures Leader if you

- ☆ love the Lord and love children;
- ☆ have a flair for drama and can play a role convincingly;
- ☆ relish a fast-paced, exciting atmosphere;
- ☆ believe in hands-on discovery as a learning technique; and
- ☆ feel comfortable facilitating group discussions.

Responsibilities

As a Blockbuster Bible Adventures Leader, you'll be responsible for

- ☆ attending scheduled leader training,
- ☆ repeating the daily Bible Point as you teach,
- ☆ collecting necessary supplies,
- ☆ recruiting three to five volunteers to perform simple roles as Bible characters,
- ☆ setting up props for Blockbuster Bible Adventures,
- ☆ leading four sessions of Blockbuster Bible Adventures each day,
- ☆ sharing props with the Show Time Leader, and
- ☆ assisting with Show Time as needed.

Related Interests

If you enjoy any of the following activities, you'll enjoy leading Blockbuster Bible Adventures:

- ★ storytelling,
- ★ acting or drama,
- ★ leading discussions, and
- ★ surprising others.

Join the cast at HolyWord Studios:

Where kids star in God's story!

Job Description

Chadder's Adventure Theater Leader

Qualifications

You'll be a successful Chadder's Adventure Theater Leader if you

- ☆ love the Lord and love children,
- ☆ have an interest in Bible study skills,
- ☆ know how to operate your church's TV and VCR,
- ☆ understand that videos can be effective learning tools for today's kids,
- ☆ enjoy facilitating group discussions, and
- ☆ ask questions to help kids connect the Bible Point they've learned in the *Chadder's HolyWord Adventure* video to their everyday lives.

Responsibilities

As a Chadder's Adventure Theater Leader, you'll be responsible for

- ☆ attending scheduled leader training,
- ☆ repeating the daily Bible Point as you teach,
- ☆ setting up a TV and VCR,
- ☆ cuing the *Chadder's HolyWord Adventure* video to each day's segment,
- ☆ helping Film Crew Leaders facilitate group discussions,
- ☆ leading four sessions of Chadder's Adventure Theater each day,
- ☆ showing the *Chadder's HolyWord Adventure* video segment to the preschoolers each day, and
- ☆ assisting with Show Time as needed.

Related Interests

If you enjoy any of the following activities, you'll enjoy leading Chadder's Adventure Theater:

- ★ watching movies,
- ★ acting or drama,
- ★ leading discussions, and
- ★ operating electronic equipment.

Join the cast at HolyWord Studios:

Where kids star in God's story!

Job Description

Show Time Leader

Qualifications

You'll be a successful Show Time Leader if you

- ☆ love the Lord and love children,
- ☆ enjoy being in front of people,
- ☆ are an expressive storyteller,
- ☆ like to laugh and have a good sense of humor, and
- ☆ can encourage and affirm kids' participation in each day's Show Time.

Responsibilities

As a Show Time Leader, you'll be responsible for

- ☆ attending scheduled leader training,
- ☆ repeating the daily Bible Point as you teach,
- ☆ collecting necessary supplies,
- ☆ setting up props for each day's Show Time,
- ☆ practicing each day's Show Time script ahead of time,
- ☆ recruiting and training other Location Leaders to assist you,
- ☆ leading Show Time for the entire HolyWord Studios each day, and
- ☆ assisting the Studio Director as needed.

Related Interests

If you enjoy any of the following activities, you'll enjoy leading Show Time:

- ★ public speaking,
- ★ acting or drama,
- ★ storytelling,
- ★ making people laugh, and
- ★ supervising teams of people.

Join the cast at HolyWord Studios:
Where kids star in God's story!

Job Description

Preschool Bible Playhouse Director

Qualifications

You'll be a successful Preschool Bible Playhouse Director if you

- ☆ love the Lord and love children;
- ☆ get down on the floor and interact with children at their eye level;
- ☆ use simple language that preschoolers can understand; and
- ☆ stock your room with blocks, dress-up clothes, modeling dough, and other age-appropriate toys and supplies.

Responsibilities

As a Preschool Bible Playhouse Director, you'll be responsible for

- ☆ attending scheduled leader training,
- ☆ repeating the daily Bible Point as you teach,
- ☆ collecting necessary supplies,
- ☆ leading a team of Film Crew Leaders for preschoolers,
- ☆ telling the daily Bible story in a fun and involving way,
- ☆ supervising preschoolers during outdoor activities, and
- ☆ leading preschoolers in singing.

Related Interests

If you enjoy any of the following activities, you'll enjoy leading Preschool Bible Playhouse:

- ★ playing with young children,
- ★ storytelling,
- ★ singing, and
- ★ being outdoors.

Join the cast at HolyWord Studios:

Where kids star in God's story!

Casting Film Crew Leaders

After you've enlisted Location Leaders, you'll need a group of Film Crew Leaders. The Film Crew Leader is an important part of each Film Crew. Anyone in your church who loves the Lord and loves children can be a Film Crew Leader! You'll need one Film Crew Leader for every five elementary-age children.

Film Crew Leaders don't have to prepare anything; they just come each day and join in the HolyWord Studios fun. Their week will go more smoothly if you have a brief orientation meeting with your Film Crew Leaders or if you invite them to your leader training meeting. The *Sneak Preview* video has a special training section just for them. It gives them helpful hints on leading discussions and solving any problems that might arise among their crews. We've also included photocopiable handouts that orient Film Crew Leaders with the teaching style at HolyWord Studios and give them some ideas for capitalizing on extra time. You can find these handouts in the leader training section of this manual (pp. 118-123).

The following guidelines will help you find top-notch Film Crew Leaders.

A Film Crew Leader is	A Film Crew Leader isn't
• a friend and a helper.	• the boss or the teacher.
• someone who offers kids choices.	• someone who makes all the decisions.
• someone who asks questions.	• someone who gives all the answers.
• someone who encourages kids.	• someone who yells at kids or puts them down.

Photocopy the "Casting Call! Be a Film Crew Leader at HolyWord Studios!" sign (p. 98), and post it in your church lobby. You'll be pleasantly surprised at how many Film Crew Leaders join your team!

HolyWord HiNtS

If Film Crew Leaders can't attend the leader training meeting, encourage them to watch the training video and review the handouts from pages 118-123. To allow plenty of time for Film Crew Leaders to understand their roles, you might consider photocopying the "For Film Crew Leaders Only" handouts from pages 118-123 several weeks before HolyWord Studios. Then staple all the information into a handy packet. Have information packets available at church, or even include the packet in your church bulletin. Your job will be much easier if Film Crew Leaders read and understand this information well before VBS begins!

Casting Call!

Be a Film Crew Leader at HolyWord Studios!

Qualifications

- Be at least fourteen years old.
- Love the Lord.
- Love children.
- Like to have fun.

Responsibilities

- Attend a leader training meeting.
- Attend HolyWord Studios each day.
- Participate in fun activities with a group of three to five elementary-age kids.

If you're interested, we'd love your autograph below, or see

____

HolyWord Studios Director

TODAY!

Name and phone number	Name and phone number

Casting Film Crew Leaders for Preschoolers

Your youngest "stars" need Film Crew Leaders, too! Like Film Crew Leaders for the elementary-age kids, Film Crew Leaders for preschoolers don't need to prepare anything in advance. In fact, their job is even easier! Instead of leading Film Crews, Film Crew Leaders for preschoolers help their Film Crews follow directions given by the Preschool Bible Playhouse Director.

Film Crew Leaders for preschoolers play with children, help them complete art projects, and keep them together when they leave the room. To ensure adequate supervision for the preschoolers who attend your HolyWord Studios, you need one Film Crew Leader for every five preschool-age children.

What kind of person would make a good Film Crew Leader for preschoolers?

A Film Crew Leader for preschoolers is

- a friend and a helper.
- someone who helps children complete activities.
- someone who gets down on the floor to interact with children.
- someone who encourages children.

A Film Crew Leader for preschoolers isn't

- the boss or the teacher.
- someone who completes children's activities for them.
- someone who supervises children from a distance.
- someone who yells at children or puts them down.

Photocopy the "Casting Call! Be a Film Crew Leader for Preschoolers at HolyWord Studios!" handout (p. 100), and post it in your church lobby. You'll be pleasantly surprised at how many Film Crew Leaders for preschoolers join your team!

Casting Call!

Be a Film Crew Leader for Preschoolers at HolyWord Studios!

Qualifications

- Be at least fourteen years old.
- Love the Lord.
- Love children.
- Like to have fun.

Responsibilities

- Attend a leader training meeting.
- Attend HolyWord Studios each day.
- Participate in fun activities with a group of three to five preschool-age children.

If you're interested, we'd love your autograph below, or see

____

HolyWord Studios Director

TODAY!

Name and phone number	Name and phone number

Casting Studio Sign-In Personnel and Registrar

It's important to have staff near the registration tables to greet, welcome, and direct children. You'll also need at least one official Registrar to make sure registration goes smoothly.

For your Registrar, look for someone who

- pays close attention to details,
- is organized,
- is familiar with many kids in your church (this helps when forming Film Crews and provides kids with a familiar face on Day 1),
- understands the "combined-age" concept, and
- meets deadlines with a cheerful spirit.

Allow the Registrar to read through the registration section of this HolyWord Studios Director Manual several weeks before HolyWord Studios is set to begin production. Be sure that all registration forms and phone registrations are given to the Registrar.

For Studio Sign-In volunteers, look for individuals who

- are friendly and outgoing,
- are comfortable interacting with children, and
- want to help with HolyWord Studios but can't commit much time.

You can have different Studio Sign-In greeters each day—kids will love the surprise! Encourage your greeters to dress up in HolyWord Studios staff T-shirts or Bible-times costumes that give clues about that day's Bible stories. Greeters can direct children to Preschool Bible Playhouse or can help kids find their Film Crew Leaders.

A Cue From Our Crew

It was wonderful to have a small crew of volunteers devoted to registration! Our directors loved handing that responsibility over to someone else, freeing them up to attend to other details! Teamwork is the way to go!

A Cue From Our Crew

Our Registration staff enlisted a few middle-schoolers to act as "ushers" who led children inside and helped them find their Film Crews. This simple step spoke volumes to parents (and kids) who were new to the church! It got everyone off to a good start...and was a wonderful way to give responsibility to middle-schoolers!

Casting a HolyWord Studios Photographer

HolyWord HiNtS

We've made it even easier for you to create a video or photo storyboard of your production. Check out the overview chart on page 10 and look for the movie camera icon next to selected activities. That icon is a "cue" for you, alerting you to a great video or photo opportunity.

HolyWord Studios will be a memorable event—one you'll want to capture on film. With today's speedy photo processing, you can make photos a fun part of your HolyWord Studios program. (You may even want the photographer to dress as a reporter, with a Press Pass tucked into the rim of a fedora! He or she can be the *paparazzi,* capturing photos of your "stars"!)

Here's how:

1. Enlist a staff Photographer. This person could be

- a parent,
- a church member,
- a friend or acquaintance from your community,
- the Sing & Play Soundtrack Leader,
- the Show Time Leader,
- your pastor or another church staff person, or
- yourself.

Your Photographer should be familiar with the camera or video equipment he or she will be using.

2. Decide whether you want to shoot slides, prints, or video. The following ideas will help you decide how to incorporate photography into your VBS.

- **Show Time slide show**—Have your Photographer visit each Location and take slide photographs of kids in action. Take the slide film to be processed. On the last day of Show Time, show slides you've taken during the week. If your Photographer is fast and if you have one-hour slide processing available, you can even have more than one slide show during the week.

- **HolyWord Studios photo frames**—During Movie Munchies, have your Photographer take two print photos of each participant (including Film Crew Leaders) and three print photos of each Film Crew. (It may take two or three days to complete this project, so start early!) Have the print film processed, and then put the photos in cardboard photo frames to sell or give away as souvenirs. Photo frames with the HolyWord Studios logo are available from Group Publishing and your local Christian bookstore.

- **HolyWord Studios premiere night**—Have your Photographer videotape kids as they visit their Locations each day. (The camera work will only add to your movie

A Cue From Our Crew

When we took Film Crew photos during our field test, the kids came up with a great idea. Several crews had worked before or after HolyWord Studios to decorate their numbered Film Crew sign, and they held up their colorful sign for their photo. Not only did the signs add a bright, personal touch to the picture, but they made it easy to figure out which Film Crew was in the photo!

studio environment!) Encourage the Photographer to interview kids about the things they're doing and what they like best. After your program, have a HolyWord Studios video night where you show the video to kids, parents, and church members.

• **HolyWord Studios photo display**—Have your Photographer take print photographs of kids in action. Then display the photographs on a poster or bulletin board in your church lobby. This is a great way to give church members a peek into HolyWord Studios. And extra photos make great outreach tools as an excuse to visit new families who sent their children to HolyWord Studios.

3. Meet with your Photographer before HolyWord Studios. Talk about the number and kinds of photos you want. Decide who will have the film processed and who will select the photos or slides you'll use.

4. Watch kids' eyes light up as they see themselves in living color!

HolyWord HiNtS

Here's another great way to involve youth in a meaningful way—enlist a real Film Crew of high-schoolers. Equip them with microphones, a video camera, and the overview chart on page 10. Be sure to explain what you want them to capture on video. Have your Film Crew interview kids and adults, catch "bloopers" (for out-takes!), and show the excitement of each day.

Extras! Filling Out Your Cast

In addition to Location Leaders, Film Crew Leaders, a Photographer, and registration staff, you may want to cast the following staff members:

• **publicity coordinator**—This person is responsible for coordinating publicity before and during your HolyWord Studios. This might include selecting publicity supplies, planning outreach publicity campaigns, inviting local TV or newspaper reporters, contacting church and community members, or arranging for community news releases. (TV coverage on Day 5 would be a super way to tell your community about Operation Kid-to-Kid!) The publicity section of this manual will help your publicity coordinator plan a great publicity campaign using the HolyWord Studios publicity supplies available from Group Publishing and your local Christian bookstore.

• **family resource coordinator**—This person is responsible for collecting the completed order forms and money for family resources, placing the order, and then distributing the items when they arrive. You may want to direct this person to the "It's a Wrap!" section of this manual (pp. 173-186).

• **transportation coordinator**—This person is responsible for coordinating transportation to and from HolyWord Studios. This might include organizing car pools, planning van or bus routes, or actually picking up children and transporting them to your facility.

HolyWord HiNtS

We've received many letters from VBS Directors who entered a VBS float in a local parade. Consider creating a float that's decorated as a Bible scene being filmed. Have kids or adults on and around the float, pretending to film (or add makeup, or touch up costumes on) the "actors." What a fun way to alert the community about your HolyWord Studios!

HolyWord HINTS

A smooth registration speaks volumes to parents and caregivers who bring their kids to your HolyWord Studios. A few volunteers who can only commit a little time make a huge difference at your registration area!

• **child-care coordinator**—This person is responsible for providing or coordinating child care for the HolyWord Studios staff. If possible, child care should be provided for all children (age two and younger) of Location Leaders and Film Crew Leaders.

• **registration workers**—You'll need a team of four to five registration workers to ensure smooth, speedy check-in on Day 1. Registration workers check in kids who have preregistered and make sure walk-in participants complete registration forms. With your guidance, registration workers also assign walk-in participants to Film Crews. Plan to meet with the registration team *before* registration to go over the registration information on pages 137-154.

• **music accompanist**—If you want to use live music during Sing & Play Soundtrack, enlist a pianist, guitarist, or even a drummer to help lead singing.

When your cast is complete, you're ready to roll those cameras!

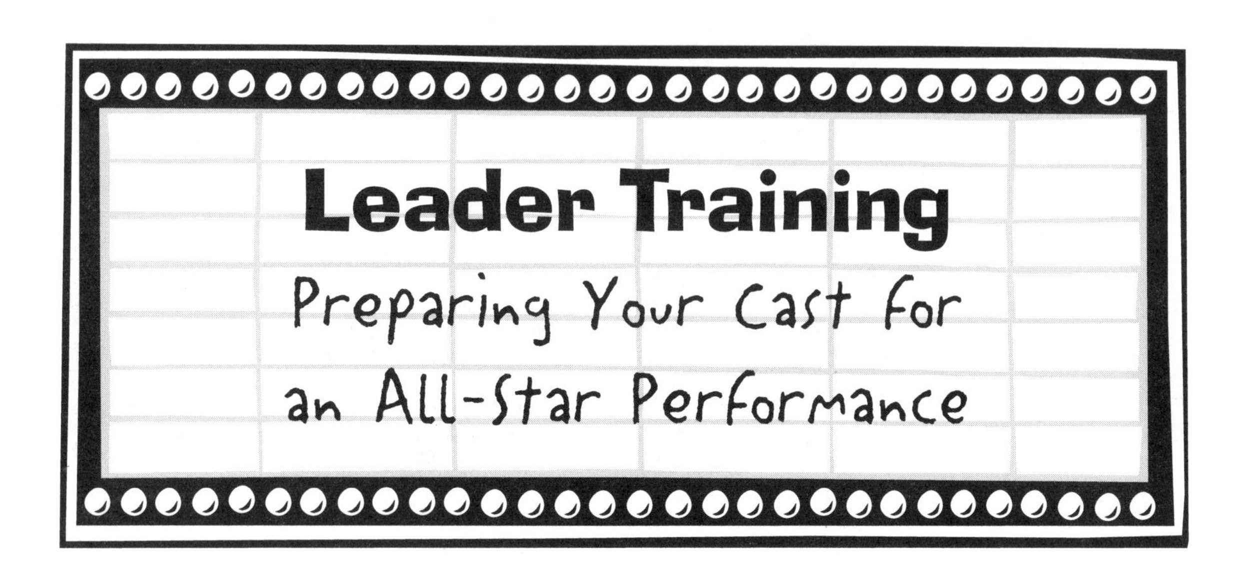

Leader Training

Preparing Your Cast for an All-Star Performance

Using the *Sneak Preview* Video

Welcome to HolyWord Studios! We're glad you've chosen HolyWord Studios for your church's VBS program. We know you're excited about presenting this blockbuster HolyWord Studios production in your community. The *Sneak Preview* video can help you get others in your church excited, too. The video is divided into two segments.

• **The promotional clip** gives a brief introduction to Group's HolyWord Studios. In this five-minute segment, you discover what makes HolyWord Studios different from other programs, and you learn how simple it is to turn your church into an exciting movie set! Your church leaders, your Christian education board, and your congregation can see kids learning the Bible Points and Bible stories each day. Show the promotional clip in your children's church or Sunday school classes to get kids excited about their starring role in God's Story. (This is a great way to get most of your kids preregistered, too!) This short "teaser" will get everyone into the action!

• **The overview and training portion** is a great tool for helping volunteers, parents, or other church members understand how HolyWord Studios works. Your Location Leaders can be reassured to see kids successfully completing the activities described in their Location Leader manuals. They'll see kids in a real HolyWord Studios program enjoying Now Playing Games, serving and tasting Movie Munchies, creating spectacular Prop Shop Crafts, and discovering Bible truths in new and meaningful ways. This segment helps Location Leaders see the "big picture" and become more confident with their roles.

This portion of the video also provides Film Crew Leaders with valuable information about their role at HolyWord Studios. Through interviews with real crew leaders from our field test, your volunteers can learn how to work with their Film Crews, discover what's expected of them, and see the impact they can have on the kids at HolyWord Studios. Film Crew Leaders even get tips on handling concerns or difficulties that might arise. Recruiting volunteers has never been simpler!

HolyWord HiNtS

The *Sneak Preview* video really does make your job easy! Your staff (or cast) will love seeing a real HolyWord Studios production in progress, and they'll be reassured that their activities really *will* be a success. This is a simple way to recruit, train, and prepare your staff.

A Cue From Our Crew

We filmed a group of Film Crew Leaders moments after each day's program had ended. This format captured the crew leaders' thoughts and feelings right away, and gave us excellent insight as to what activities and experiences had risen to the top. You may want to gather a group of Film Crew Leaders each day and ask them to give advice to future VBS volunteers. Compile these interviews with VBS footage to create a promotional "trailer" for your 2001 program! You'll be amazed at how these real-life "stars" will help with training and recruiting next year's staff.

"Lights, Camera, Action!" Leader Training Meeting

A Cue From Our Crew

The staff T-shirts and Film Crew Leader caps were a huge success! Not only did they help identify staff and leaders, they were a nice "thank you" to those who had "starring roles" in our production!

HolyWord HiNtS

The *Sing & Play Soundtrack Music Video* lets volunteers see Sing & Play Soundtrack fun in action! This video (available from Group Publishing and your local Christian bookstore) is a super way to add enthusiasm, build confidence, and teach all thirteen HolyWord Studios songs.

HolyWord HiNtS

Before your meeting, watch the *Sneak Preview* video. Note the places where you'll stop the video to invite teachers to try out actual HolyWord Studios activities. If your VCR has a counter, you may even want to jot down the counter number for each stopping place in the margin of this manual.

You'll need the following supplies:

Things you can find around your home:

- a Bible
- scissors
- a cassette or CD player
- masking tape
- a permanent marker

Things you can find around your church:

- name tags
- a TV and a VCR
- chairs
- two tables
- paper cups
- juice or water
- plastic knives
- paper plates
- napkins
- markers
- bowl
- spoons

Things you'll find in your Starter Kit:

- the *Sing & Play Soundtrack* audiocassette
- the Elementary Student Book
- the *Sneak Preview* video
- the HolyWord Studios leader manuals

Things you'll need to collect or purchase:

- large sheets of poster board (one per Film Crew)
- the *Sing & Play Soundtrack Music Video** (optional)
- the *Chadder's HolyWord Adventure* video*
- a hand clapper* or another attention-getting signal
- HolyWord Studios staff T-shirts* (optional)
- Film Crew Leader caps* (optional)
- two containers of white frosting
- food coloring (your choice of colors)
- two resealable plastic bags
- one cupcake for each participant
- rainbow sprinkles
- licorice ropes, such as Red Vines (not thin licorice whips)
- trash cans
- photocopies of the "For Film Crew Leaders Only" handouts (pp. 118-123)
- paper or Mylar stars (optional)
- directors chair (optional)
- Bible movie posters* (optional)

*These items are available from Group Publishing and your local Christian bookstore.

Before the meeting, set up a TV and a VCR in your meeting room. Set up chairs facing the TV. In the back of the room, set up two tables. Then decorate your meeting room by hanging paper or Mylar stars from the ceiling, setting a directors chair in the front of the room, and posting the Bible movie posters around the room (these are available from Group Publishing or your local Christian bookstore). You may want to rent a popcorn machine and have tantalizing, buttery popcorn for "cast members" to munch as they mingle. To make your meeting room even more "epic," try some of the decorating ideas beginning on page 58, or in the catalog in the Starter Kit.

Scoop the contents of one container of white frosting into a resealable plastic bag. Add a few drops of food coloring, seal the bag securely, and be sure to squeeze out as much air as possible. Then knead the contents until the color is thoroughly mixed in. Press the contents into one corner of the bag and set it aside. Repeat the process with the other container of frosting, but add a different color of food coloring. Place one bag at each table.

Set a stack of paper plates, napkins, cups, juice or water, and one plate of cupcakes at the end of each table, near the bags of frosting. Set the packages of licorice ropes in the middle of each table, near a couple of plastic knives. Then place a bowl of rainbow sprinkles and at least two spoons at the end of the table. Be sure to have a few trash cans nearby.

Create an informative "HolyWord Hints" packet for each of your Film Crew Leaders to keep. Include photocopies of the "For Film Crew Leaders Only" handouts (pp. 118-123), a sample daily schedule, as well as a list of Location Leader names. Pass out the packets to your Film Crew Leaders at the end of the meeting. (You may also want to include the "Helping Children Follow Jesus" handout on page 175 of this Director Manual.)

A Cue From Our Crew

We wrote the movie "roles" on 1x3-inch file folder labels. These were easy to work with, but didn't stick well to people's clothing. We recommend plain old sticky masking tape for this activity.

Set a large sheet of poster board under each chair, along with a pair of scissors, and a handful of markers. Place name tags and markers near your entryway. On wide strips of masking tape, clearly write the following movie "roles":

- actor
- sound technician
- makeup artist
- costume designer
- producer
- script writer
- set designer
- lighting technician
- special effects expert
- camera operator

It's fine to duplicate the number of these roles, as long as you have one role for each participant. Attach the strips of tape around one of the tables or somewhere near the doorway.

Play the *Sing & Play Soundtrack* audiocassette or CD as volunteers arrive. Greet each Film Crew Leader or Location Leader with a warm smile. Encourage each volunteer to create a name tag before sitting down. While participants are making their name tags, stick one of the "roles" on each person's back, but don't tell him or her what the role is. As others arrive, encourage your cast members to interact and give one another clues about the role they've just been given. Be sure to thank everyone for coming to this meeting and for helping with HolyWord Studios.

When everyone has arrived, gradually turn down the volume of the *Sing & Play Soundtrack* audiocassette or CD, and then stop the cassette or CD player. Shake your hand clapper or use another attention-getting signal. Say: **Let's get the cameras rolling on this epic production! My name is** [name], **and I'll be your Studio Director. It's great to have each one of you on our HolyWord Studios cast and crew. Let's start our training time with a prayer.**

Pray: **Dear God, thank you for each person here; they're all important members of this program. Thank you for their willing hearts and their desire to help children get a better picture of your amazing story. Guide our time together, and help us remember that each child at our VBS is a star in your eyes. In Jesus' name, amen.**

Say: **Before we get into the real "action" at HolyWord Studios, I'd like you to find a partner sitting near you and introduce yourself. Your partner may give one more clue about the role I placed on your back earlier. After you've each guessed your "identity," reach around and remove the tape from your back. Then tell the real role you'll be playing in our HolyWord Studios production.** Pause while volunteers talk about their real and pretend roles. After thirty seconds, shake your hand clapper to regain everyone's attention. Say: **This is my hand clapper—it's like getting your own round of applause every time I shake it! I'll shake the hand clapper to give you a round of applause whenever I need your attention. I'll also use it each day of our HolyWord Studios to let you know when it's time to dismiss your kids to their next Location. Location Leaders, you may want to use your own hand clappers at HolyWord Studios. Each day is overflowing with activities, so you won't want to lose a minute!** Then ask:

- **What are some of the parts I assigned to each of you?**

Say: **It sure takes a lot of different people to make a movie, doesn't it? Just as it takes a variety of people to create a movie, our VBS needs a variety of people with special gifts and talents. God can use all of us in this production—whether we're behind the scenes or in front of the "camera," we're all an important part of this program.**

Continue: **HolyWord Studios is where kids star in God's story!** Hold up a Bible. **All of God's story is important to these young stars. Turn to a different partner and talk about which "scene" from God's story you hope children really grasp during their time here. Maybe it's a verse that's been meaningful to you, or a story that you think would touch their hearts and lives. You'll have about thirty seconds to share.**

After a few seconds, say: **Let's begin our *Sneak Preview* video to see why HolyWord Studios is such an exciting program.**

Start the *Sneak Preview* video, and show the short promotional clip. Continue into the overview portion of the video.

After the host says, "And crew jobs boost self-esteem as kids star in God's amazing story," stop the VCR.

Say: **If you'll be a Film Crew Leader or Assistant Film Crew Leader during HolyWord Studios, please stand.** Invite Film Crew Leaders to introduce themselves; then give all the Film Crew Leaders and assistants a round of applause. Continue: **Without Film Crew Leaders, HolyWord Studios would never make it into production! We're looking forward to epic adventures and blockbuster Bible fun with your help. To prepare you for your role, I'm going to give each of you a Film Crew Leader cap to wear this week. This is sort of like your "costume" in the HolyWord Studios production. Your caps will help me, the kids, and the Location Leaders find you more easily.** Give a crew leader cap to each Film Crew Leader and Assistant Film Crew Leader.

Continue the video. You'll hear the host talk about Locations.

After the host says, "Because most Locations operate simultaneously, you'll prepare just twenty-five minutes of material that you'll present up to four times each day as groups of children visit your Location," stop the VCR.

Say: **If you'll be a Location Leader during HolyWord Studios, please stand up.**

HolyWord HiNtS

If you're providing attention-getting signals for your Location Leaders, this would be a good time to distribute them. You can use hand clappers, available from Group Publishing and your local Christian bookstore, or any other noisemaker of your choice. (Kids will love them!)

A Cue From Our Crew

Film Crew Leader caps were a popular item! We quickly ran out and wished we'd ordered more for the additional crew leaders who joined the team. These hats make it easy for you (and Location Leaders) to identify crew leaders, and are a fun "name tag," as well!

HolyWord HiNtS

It's a good idea to open up one of the bandage wrappers so everyone can see that "God Loves You" is printed in three different languages. You'll help your crew see that they'll have a far-reaching impact with this program.

HolyWord HiNtS

If you'll be focusing on Operation Kid-to-Kid in your community, you may want to provide more information on the area where you'll distribute the Care Kits.

HolyWord HiNtS

If your entire staff made it to the meeting, pat yourself on the back! Now you have extra hands to create the preschool signs! Preschoolers join Film Crews that have color names, rather than numbers; for example, Yellow Stars, Blue Stars, or Red Stars. Ask several volunteers to cut large stars from colored poster board (which is more durable than construction paper) and decorate these stars with glitter, wiggly-eyes, or other fun craft items.

Invite Location Leaders to introduce themselves, and tell which Location they'll be leading. Say: **Location Leaders will help direct kids as they star in God's story. In fact, kids will study God's amazing story every day as they use their Student Books.** Hold up an Elementary Student Book. Say: **At HolyWord Studios, elementary kids use an actual Gospel of Matthew to learn how to read, understand, and apply Bible truths to their lives. They'll see that the Bible is like a script that guides them through life. All kids—elementary and preschool—will use specially designed stickers to mark key passages in their Bibles. After HolyWord Studios, kids can go back and easily find those verses and apply them to everyday situations.**

Continue the video. You'll hear the host explain how everything at HolyWord Studios reinforces the Bible Point. Then you'll hear the host talk about Operation Kid-to-Kid.

Stop the VCR after the host says, "They'll see that they have an important role in showing God's love to others."

Say: **As kids are starring in God's story, they'll also play an important role in sharing God's love through Operation Kid-to-Kid. Kids will get a start on their Care Kits, simply by opening their Student Books. Inside, they'll discover four specially printed adhesive bandages.** Open a Student Book and show the Operation Kid-to-Kid adhesive bandages. Say: **Kids will add two of the "God Loves You" bandages, along with other health items such as a toothbrush, a comb, or a washcloth to a Care Kit. At the end of the week, we'll present our Care Kits as an offering, and then send them out for worldwide distribution.**

Let's take a few minutes and see what an impact the kids in our community can have. Under your chair, you'll find a sheet of poster board, scissors, and a few markers. These are supplies to create the Film Crew signs for elementary crews. The signs will help kids know where their crews are gathering during Sing & Play Soundtrack and Show Time. We'll go around the room and count off, so each person has a number. Cut your poster board into a large star, then write your number really big on one side of your poster board. Make it huge and clear, so kids can see it from a distance. Then take a moment to decorate the sign in a colorful, creative way.

Lead the group in counting off; then allow five minutes for individuals to write their numbers and decorate the crew signs. (You may want to have Location Leaders decorate their door signs at this time.)

Say: **Now, take a minute and silently pray for the kids in that crew. Pray also for one preschool crew. Ask God to guide their time and to help them find delight in God's amazing story.**

Pause while volunteers silently pray, and then say: **Amen. Now, gather with three or four others and form a circle.** Pause while volunteers form groups. Say: **Each person in your group represents one elementary or preschool crew of**

about five kids. Place one of your hands in the middle of the circle to show the five kids you're representing—one for each finger. Pause, then say: **Each of your groups also represents one needy child who will receive a Care Kit, due to our program. In your groups, pray aloud for the children in other countries who will receive a symbol of God's love and care.**

Pause while volunteers pray, then say: **Amen. Go ahead and tuck the crew sign under your chair, and then have a seat. Let's return to our video to preview more about HolyWord Studios.**

Continue the video. You'll see children making snacks for the entire HolyWord Studios cast and crew.

When you hear the Movie Munchies Leader say, "I couldn't tear them away from the tables," stop the VCR.

Say: **Let's visit the snack bar and make one of the snacks kids will make at Movie Munchies. We'll make Mini Birthday Cakes—a snack to remind kids on Day 5 that Pentecost was the birthday of the church. During HolyWord Studios, Film Crew Leaders help with snack preparation by handling sharp knives, pouring juice, and helping kids find jobs they do well. Let's have our Film Crew Leaders be "drink-pourers" and "licorice-cutters."**

We'll all work in an assembly line to make our treats. Some helpers will frost the cupcakes, using the handy "pastry bags" I've set out. Then other helpers will sprinkle rainbow sprinkles on each cupcake. Film Crew Leaders will cut the licorice sticks into three sections to create "candles." Then another helper will push a licorice candle into the center of each cupcake. Hold up a finished snack so everyone can see how each cupcake should look. Say: **When we've made a Mini Birthday Cake and a drink for each person, grab a treat, and find a seat near two other people.**

Play the *Sing & Play Soundtrack* audiocassette or CD while volunteers create snacks. When everyone is enjoying a snack, say: **Each Birthday Cake is a reminder that we can celebrate God's presence with us. Turn to a partner, and tell him or her one way we can see God's presence here at VBS.**

After a minute or two, shake your hand clapper, and allow a few volunteers to share their responses. Then say: **In Matthew 5:16, Jesus says, "In the same way, let your light shine before men, that they may see your good deeds and praise your Father in heaven." You will be stars this week, shining God's love through your words and actions. Just as the Birthday Cakes were sweet reminders of God's presence, you can be sweet reminders of God to the children here at**

A Cue From Our Crew

Originally we asked the trainees to simply write the number, without decorating it. But most of them took off and made cool, creative, colorful signs! Several volunteers asked to stay afterward and finish decorating their signs. You'll love seeing how "artsy" this group can be. Plus, your program will look super!

A Cue From Our Crew

Prayer is such a tremendous way to prepare your crew! We discovered that these various ways to pray not only gave staff members a chance to commit their week to God, but gave them an opportunity to come together as a team. Even if you need to trim time from your meeting, be sure to include plenty of time for corporate prayer!

HolyWord Studios. Let's take a sneak preview at some more coming attractions!

Continue the video. You'll hear about Now Playing Games and how they help children remember the daily Point.

Stop the VCR when you hear, "The kids really make the connection."

Say: **During HolyWord Studios, even the games help children learn more about God's love! When kids work together at Now Playing Games, they learn that following God can be like an action movie—filled with movement, activity, and excitement! Let's get up and try out one of our Now Playing Games! This game is played on Day 2, when children are learning about how God protected the Israelites during the plagues.**

Gather with about five other people and form a circle on the ground. This game is similar to the old favorite, Telephone. You'll take turns passing a message around the circle, whispering the message to each other. While you're passing the message, one of your group members will be a gnat, buzzing loudly in each group member's ear. Take a few seconds to choose your roles, then begin.

> **A Cue From Our Crew**
>
> *Group discussion and pair shares are a super way to get everyone involved and participating. We discovered that by practicing group discussion in leader training, our Film Crew Leaders were better prepared to use these techniques with kids.*

Allow about thirty seconds for groups to form, choose roles, and begin. Every minute or so, call out for group members to change roles. After each group member has had a turn to be a gnat, shake your hand clapper and get everyone's attention.

Say: **In your groups, be sure you're sitting so you can see everyone. During HolyWord Studios, when you discuss questions with your Film Crew, be sure kids are facing each other. This is the best way to promote good communication! Now talk about these questions.** Ask:

- **What was it like to have the gnat buzzing in your ear?**
- **What distractions keep us from hearing God's words for us?**
- **What distractions might keep children from learning more about God's love this week?**

> **A Cue From Our Crew**
>
> *This was a great opportunity for adults and teenagers to start working together as a team. Not only did it allow everyone to get acquainted (and have lots of fun), but it was a hands-on example of the way they'd be helping kids in the coming week!*

Say: **In your group, come up with a few solutions to keep kids focused on growing in their relationship with Jesus. For example, if kids get distracted by talking to their friends, you might let kids practice telling their friends about Jesus.** Allow a few minutes for groups to brainstorm. Use the hand clapper to call time, then ask a few groups to share their ideas.

Then say: **In your groups, take a moment to silently pray for the kids who will come to VBS. Ask that God will focus their hearts and attention on him.**

Pause a moment for silent prayer; then continue.

Say: **Let's learn more about HolyWord Studios with our *Sneak Preview* video.**

Continue the *Sneak Preview* video and watch as children explore exciting Bible adventures during Blockbuster Bible Adventures.

Stop the VCR when you hear the leader say, "And I think, what better thing could you do than engross kids in a Bible story."

Say: **Participating in each activity is a great way to encourage kids to join in the fun, too. Turn to a partner—sit knee to knee so you can see each other—and tell three ways you can participate during HolyWord Studios. For example, you could sing and do motions at Sing & Play Soundtrack or have fun with Now Playing Games.**

Allow two minutes for partners to share, and then say: **I'd like to hear some of the ideas you came up with.** Allow several people to share, then say: **Your example and enthusiasm will set the stage for kids to grow in their relationship with Jesus. As kids at HolyWord Studios follow your lead, they'll discover the joy and fun of following God! Now let's return to our video to see what else is in store for us at HolyWord Studios.**

Continue the video. You'll hear how fun and easy it is to lead Sing & Play Soundtrack, as well as the exciting dramas at Show Time.

Stop the VCR after you hear, "They've had a great time with music especially."

You'll also hear more about Prop Shop Crafts. You'll learn about unforgettable crafts, such as the TLSeed Necklace, Yahoo Yo-Yos, and Amazing Pictures. Then you'll hear about Chadder's Adventure Theater and will discover how preschoolers will be involved in HolyWord Studios.

Stop the VCR after you hear the host say, "And we've worked out all the bloopers so the snacks are easy to prepare...even for small hands."

Say: **As you can tell, everyone gets in the action at HolyWord Studios! So children (and Film Crew Leaders) will enjoy some downtime while they watch a screening of *Chadder's HolyWord Adventure*. Let's have a little preview of one of Chadder's adventures.**

Play the first five minutes of the *Chadder's HolyWord Adventure* video to give everyone a taste of what's in store. Then stop the VCR, eject the cassette, and give it to the Chadder's Adventure Theater Leader. Say: **Chadder has an amazing way of reaching everyone—from preschoolers to elementary kids—and helping them apply the Bible Point to everyday life.**

Blockbuster movies are known for behind-the-scenes glitches that surprise everyone. Rainstorms delay filming, actors get sick, and special effects don't work as planned. Our HolyWord Studios production is likely to have some unexpected surprises, too. Get together with a person sitting near you. Think of three challenges that might arise during the week.

Allow a moment for pairs to brainstorm, and then ask: **What are some of the bloopers that might happen this week?** Take a few responses, then say: **Although we might see those things as problems, God can turn any situation into**

HolyWord HINTS

If your Sing & Play Soundtrack Leader is willing, this is a good time to have him or her come up and teach the motions and chorus of "God's Story."

something valuable. Just as many films now include their outtakes, we can laugh and learn from the mistakes and challenges we face at VBS. Suggest simple solutions to the "twists and turns" mentioned. **Let's offer our concerns to God.**

Pray: **Dear God, we know that you are in charge at HolyWord Studios. You've chosen certain children to come and will allow certain situations to arise. Guide us as we deal with your children. Help us to see them with your eyes and to love them with your heart. Use us to display your love in any situation. In Jesus' name, amen.**

Continue the video. You'll hear about what a Film Crew Leader is and isn't, and hear how Film Crew Leaders in a real HolyWord Studios program solved difficulties within their Film Crews. When the tape is over, stop the VCR.

Say: **In Hollywood, famous movie stars put their hand prints in cement along Hollywood's Walk of Fame. These impressions are left for people to see for years to come. This week at VBS will leave an impression on kids' lives for many years to come. Turn over your paper star and trace your hand print on the back.** Pause while volunteers trace around their hands.

Then continue: **Now, on each finger of that hand, jot down one word that describes something you hope children will take away from their time at HolyWord Studios. You might write "love" in hopes that children will sense God's love. Or maybe you'll write "friendship," as you desire for kids to grow closer to each other.** Pause while volunteers write on their paper hands.

After about thirty seconds, say: **Matthew 19:13-15 says, "Then little children were brought to Jesus for him to place his hands on them and pray for them. But the disciples rebuked those who brought them. Jesus said, 'Let the little children come to me, and do not hinder them, for the kingdom of heaven belongs to such as these.' When he had placed his hands on them, he went on from there."**

This week, your hands will be Jesus' hands—patting a lonely child on the back, clapping in praise, drawing in a child for a hug, pointing out important messages in God's Word, and touching their hearts with God's love. Your acceptance and love will mean so much to the children you touch.

Pray: **Dear God, thank you for the volunteers you've brought here. Thank you that they have the desire to touch children's lives with your love and acceptance. Bless our week at HolyWord Studios. Give us energy and love that will help children realize that they are all stars in your eyes. Amen.**

Distribute the leader manuals to the Location Leaders, and Film Crew Leader information packets to Film Crew Leaders as they leave. Remind Film Crew Leaders to wear their caps to registration. If you purchased HolyWord Studios staff T-shirts for your Location Leaders, hand them out with the leader manuals.

HolyWord HINTS

The hand print and words on the back of each star will help Film Crew Leaders remember their goal in reaching the hearts and lives of children. It's a great way to focus on their role in sharing God's love during a busy week.

HolyWord HINTS

You may want to photocopy the age-level information sheets (on page 25 of this manual and page 18 of the Preschool Bible Playhouse Director Manual) to add to your Film Crew Leader packets.

While your HolyWord Studios crew is assembled, it's a good idea to take care of lots of "housekeeping" items. You might want to use the clip art on page 130 (or on the *Sing & Play Soundtrack Music & Clip Art CD*) to create a "HolyWord Hints" handout. Be sure to include the following:

• Tell your staff what time to arrive on the first day and where to meet. If you're planning to have staff devotions, let your staff know so they can arrive early. Be sure they know meeting times and places each day after that, as well.

• Distribute a map that shows where each Location will be (the *Sing & Play Soundtrack Music & Clip Art CD* contains spectacular clip art to help you create a map.)

• Give a complete list of names and phone numbers of Location Leaders, registration staff, and VBS Director(s).

• Inform Location Leaders and Film Crew Leaders of procedures you'll follow if there's a fire or another emergency.

For Film Crew Leaders Only

What's a Film Crew Leader?

If you've been asked to be a Film Crew Leader, you've met two important qualifications: You love the Lord, and you love kids.

During HolyWord Studios, you'll visit different Locations with a group of three to five kids. **You're not in charge of preparing or teaching activities—you just get to be there and enjoy them as part of your Film Crew!**

The following guidelines will help you be an "all-star" Film Crew Leader!

A Film Crew Leader is

- a friend and a helper.
- someone who knows and calls kids by name.
- someone who offers kids choices.
- someone who asks questions.
- someone who encourages kids.

A Film Crew Leader isn't

- the boss or the teacher.
- someone who makes all the decisions.
- someone who gives all the answers.
- someone who yells at kids or puts them down.

When talking with kids,

say,

- Let's keep moving so we can do as many fun activities as possible.
- Listen carefully so you'll know what to do next.
- Stay with the Film Crew; we need your help in this activity!
- That's a unique way of doing things! How did you think of that? Let's try it this way.
- It's important that we all follow the instructions and work together as a team.
- Please move over here so you can see better.

don't say,

- Stop talking and get back to work.
- Be quiet and listen!
- Don't run around the room.
- You're doing it wrong!
- Don't do that!
- Stay out of that area!

For Film Crew Leaders Only

Most of the time, things will go really smoothly for your Film Crew, but every once in a while, you may run into a dilemma. Here's some advice on how to handle different challenges.

If My Crew Won't Stay Together

Encourage your Studio Guide to come up with creative ways to travel. Build excitement by saying, "Our Studio Guide came up with a really cool way to get to the next Location! Let's see if we can get there quickly while we do this."

Encourage Film Crew spirit by working with your Cheerleader to come up with cheers to say as you travel.

If Older Kids Complain About Being With Younger Ones

Highlight their helping role. Encourage them to help younger kids with crafts and other activities. Acknowledge them by telling younger kids, "[Name of older child] is really good at that. Why don't you ask him (or her) to help?"

If I Have a Clique in My Crew

Cliques can make the Film Crew experience unhappy for the outsiders. Encourage friendships between all crew members by pairing kids with partners they don't know very well during games and crafts.

If a Crew Member Won't Participate

Help shy children feel welcome by calling them by name often and asking them questions directly. Respond to their questions with a smile and an encouraging statement such as, "That's really interesting" or "Wow! I bet that made you feel special!" Also, try giving children special jobs. For example, assign them the task of finding a place for your crew to sit at each Location.

If someone doesn't want to participate in Now Playing Games, that's OK. HolyWord Studios can be tiring! Let children rest until they're ready to participate. Chances are, when kids see how much fun everyone else is having, they'll want to join in, too.

If People in My Crew Don't Get Along

Quietly take the children aside. Tell them you've noticed they're not getting along. Let them know that although they don't have to be best friends, they do have to be together all week, so things will be a lot more fun if they can at least be kind to one another. (Use the daily Bible Points for these teachable moments!)

If I Have an Overly Active Child

Pair this child up with yourself during partner activities, and suggest that he or she sit with you during quiet times. Try to make sitting still a game by saying, "Let's see how long you can sit still without interrupting. I'm timing you. Ready? Go!"

If the child is really uncontrollable, ask your director if you could have an Assistant Film Crew Leader.

With a little patience and humor, you and your Film Crew can have a blockbuster experience at HolyWord Studios!

For Film Crew Leaders Only

Who's Who in the Film Crew?

During their first Sing & Play Soundtrack session, kids will choose Film Crew jobs and will place job stickers (from the HolyWord Studios sticker sheets) on their name badges. Each child will have one of the jobs listed in the chart below.

- If your crew has fewer than five kids, some kids may have more than one job.
- If your crew has more than five kids, let kids share jobs.
- If children can't agree on who should perform each job, tell them that everyone will get a chance to do all the jobs. Assign kids jobs for Day 1; then rotate jobs each day so that by the end of the week, all children in the crew have had an opportunity to do each job. Kids can simply affix a different job sticker to their name badges each day.

Kids are excited about having special jobs! Encourage them to fulfill their roles, and provide lots of opportunities for them to do so.

Reader		• likes to read • reads Bible passages aloud
Studio Guide		• chooses action ideas for traveling between Locations (shuffling, skipping, hopping, galloping, or marching) • serves as line leader to guide crew through daily schedule
Materials Manager		• likes to pass out and collect supplies • carries Film Crew bag • passes out and collects Prop Shop Crafts materials • passes out Student Books
Cheerleader		• likes to smile and make people happy • makes sure people use kind words and actions • leads group in cheering during Now Playing Games
Prayer Person		• likes to pray and isn't afraid to pray aloud • makes sure the crew takes time to pray each day • leads or opens prayer times

For Film Crew Leaders Only

What Do Film Crew Leaders Do at Each Location?

Sing & Play Soundtrack is where kids warm up for the day by singing upbeat action songs. Your job at Sing & Play Soundtrack is to

- arrive a few minutes early;
- greet your crew members in your designated seating area;
- follow the motions and sing out loud; and
- remember that if you get involved, the kids will too!

Blockbuster Bible Adventures is where kids hear the Bible story. Your job at Blockbuster Bible Adventures is to

- line up with your crew outside the door,
- ask how crew leaders should help out that day,
- keep your crew together until you receive other directions, and
- encourage crew members to participate.

Prop Shop Crafts is where kids make cool crafts and learn about Operation Kid-to-Kid™. Your job at Prop Shop Crafts is to

- listen carefully to the instructions because you will most likely need to repeat them for some members of your crew,
- help kids make their crafts (*when* they need help), and
- help clean up your area before leaving.

Now Playing Games is where kids play team-building games. Your job at Now Playing Games is to

- listen carefully to the instructions so you can help your crew members follow them,
- perform any tasks the games leader assigns to you, and
- participate in each activity and cheer on your crew members as they participate!

Movie Munchies is where crews come for a tasty snack. Your job at Movie Munchies is to

- gather your crew in a designated area,
- quiet kids and help them focus on the Movie Munchies Leader as he or she explains the snack,
- talk with kids about their experiences at VBS that day, and
- help kids clean up your area before leaving.

Chadder's Adventure Theater is where children watch *Chadder's HolyWord Adventure* and interact with their Student Book Gospels of Matthew. Your job at Chadder's Adventure Theater is to

- encourage kids to sit still and listen to the video,
- lead your crew in participating in the activities after the video,
- lead kids in discussion when it's called for, and
- help kids find and mark Bible verses.

Show Time is an exciting review of the day's lesson. Your role at Show Time is to

- lead kids to your assigned seating area,
- participate in singing and other activities,
- remind your crew to participate without being rowdy or disruptive,
- make sure each child leaves with his or her craft, and
- collect kids' name badges as they leave and store them in your Film Crew bag.

For Film Crew Leaders for Preschoolers Only

What's a Film Crew Leader for Preschoolers?

If you've been asked to be a Film Crew Leader for preschoolers, you've met two important qualifications: You love the Lord, and you love children.

During HolyWord Studios, you'll visit different Locations with a group of three to five children. **You're not in charge of preparing or teaching activities—you just get to be there and enjoy them as part of your Film Crew!**

The following guidelines will help you be an "all-star" Film Crew Leader!

A Film Crew Leader for preschoolers is

- a friend and helper.
- someone who helps children complete activities.
- someone who gets down on the floor to interact with children.
- someone who encourages kids.

A Film Crew Leader for preschoolers isn't

- the boss or the teacher.
- someone who completes children's activities for them.
- someone who supervises children from a distance.
- someone who yells at kids or puts them down.

During HolyWord Studios, you'll shepherd a group of up to five preschool children. Your role is to love, encourage, and enjoy the children in your crew. If you've never worked with preschoolers before, the following tips will help you.

- Learn the names of the children in your crew. Call children by name often.
- You'll have three-, four-, and five-year-olds in your Film Crew. You'll probably notice big differences in motor skills (such as cutting and coloring) between older and younger children. Help children work at their own pace, and encourage five-year-olds to help younger children when possible.
- Look into preschoolers' eyes when you speak to them. You may need to kneel or sit on the floor to do this.
- Empower children by offering them choices. Ask, "Would you like to make a craft or play with blocks?" Don't ask "What do you want to do?" or children may decide they want to do an activity that's unavailable or inappropriate.

For Film Crew Leaders for Preschoolers Only

As a Film Crew Leader for Preschoolers, You'll Be Expected to

• arrive at least ten minutes early each day. Report to the Preschool Bible Playhouse area (Day 1) or the Sing & Play Soundtrack area (Days 2 through 5), and be ready to greet children who arrive early. Your welcoming presence will bring smiles to anxious faces!

• greet each child by name and with a warm smile. Help children put on their name badges each day.

• keep track of your crew members' Student Books. Store these in a Film Crew bag, and place the bag in a convenient location in your classroom or church.

• sit with the children in your crew during group activities.

• accompany children to Location stations. Read the instructions at each station, and help children complete the activities. Distribute supplies from the children's books or sticker sheets as needed.

• repeat the daily Bible Point often. The more children hear or say the Bible Point, the more likely they are to remember it and apply it to their lives.

• always check to make sure all children are accounted for before leaving the Playhouse! Be sure children hold hands or a rope as you travel.

(Never grab, pinch, or pull children as you travel. If a child lags behind, remind him or her to stay with the crew. You may want to walk behind your crew so you can keep all the children in view and avoid traveling too fast.)

• report any potential discipline problems to the Playhouse Director. He or she will help you handle problems appropriately.

• sit with your crew during Show Time. Help children participate in each day's show.

• collect children's name badges after each day's Show Time.

• help children collect their Student Book Activity Pages and crafts before they leave.

• release children only to a designated parent or caregiver. If an unfamiliar adult comes to pick up a child, refer the adult to the Playhouse Director.

• assist the Playhouse Director with cleanup and preparation for your next meeting.

Thanks for joining the HolyWord Studios cast!

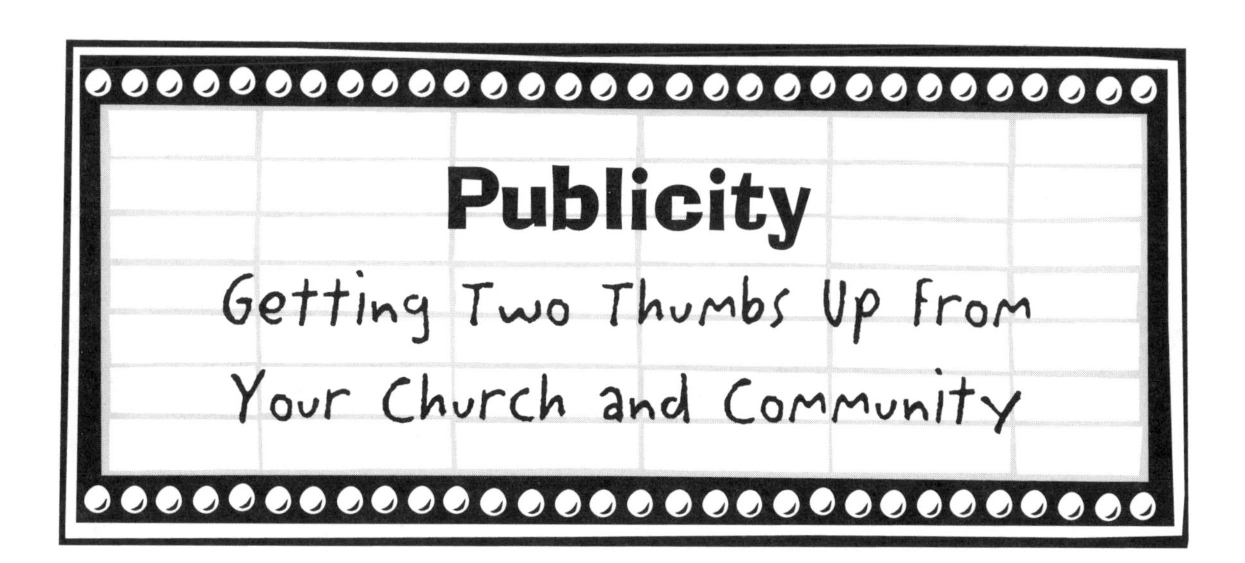
Publicity
Getting Two Thumbs Up From
Your Church and Community

Promoting HolyWord Studios in Your Church and Community

You've planned, prepared, recruited, and trained. You've assembled an all-star cast for your HolyWord Studios production. Now it's time to promote your program. Use the publicity items described below to give parents and kids in your church and your community a sneak preview of the fun that awaits them at HolyWord Studios!

In this section of your HolyWord Studios Director Manual, you'll find the following resources:

- **HolyWord Studios clip art**—Use the photocopiable clip art on page 130 to create your own custom promotional materials. You can make your own letterhead, memos, transparencies, and more!

- **HolyWord Studios bulletin inserts**—Distribute information to everyone who attends your church. Just tear out the bulletin inserts on page 131, type in your church's information, photocopy the inserts, and slip the copies into your church bulletins. To help you conserve paper, we've included two bulletin inserts on a single page.

- **Invitation to parents**—Fill in your church's information; then photocopy and mail the parent letter on page 132. If you want to personalize the letter, make any desired changes, and then transfer the letter to your church's letterhead. You can mail the letter to parents in your church or your community.

- **News release**—Adapt the news release on page 133 to fit your church's program. Then submit typed, double-spaced copies to local newspapers, radio stations, and TV stations.

- **Community flier**—Photocopy the flier on page 134, and post copies in local libraries, restaurants, grocery stores, self-service laundries, parks, recreation

HolyWord HINTS

Thanks to technology, you'll find much more clip art on the *Sing & Play Soundtrack Music & Clip Art CD.* Use your computer expertise or involve a volunteer computer whiz to help you create dazzling publicity items, scene patterns for sets, or jazz up your church's Web site.

A Cue From Our Crew

When we sent our news release to the local paper, the newspaper printed it as "Holywood Studios." Although our copy was correct, the editor at the paper must have thought we'd made a mistake. Be sure to add a note that your title is "HolyWord" not "Holywood." It's a way to bring attention to the Bible, God's Holy Word!

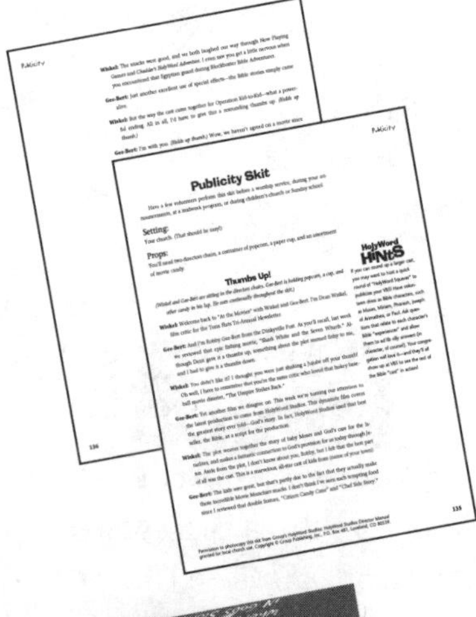
Publicity Skit

Setting:

Props:

Thumbs Up!

HolyWord Hints

centers, banks, shopping malls, and schools. Be sure to get permission before posting the fliers. You may also want to check with church members who own businesses in your community. They may be willing to post fliers at their businesses—and they may even suggest additional business owners you can contact.

• **Publicity Skit**—Ask for volunteers to perform this publicity skit (pp. 135-136) for you church congregation. The skit will give everyone a preview of the fun and excitement they can be a part of at HolyWord Studios.

The following items are also available to help you publicize your HolyWord Studios. Refer to your HolyWord Studios catalog for illustrations and prices.

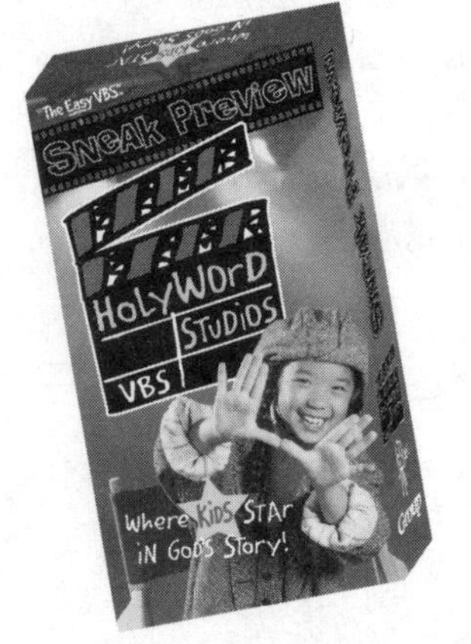

• ***Sneak Preview* video**—You may have already previewed this video when you examined your HolyWord Studios Starter Kit. In addition to being a great leader training resource, *Sneak Preview* provides you with a "teaser" (also known as a "trailer") to show to your congregation. This short video clip gives church members a sneak peek at colorful Prop Shop Crafts, marvelous Movie Munchies, and exciting Bible learning that will take place at HolyWord Studios! Plus the video explains more about Operation Kid-to-Kid, the exciting mission project your kids will take part in.

• **HolyWord Studios T-shirts**—Invite HolyWord Studios cast members to wear their staff T-shirts to church events in the weeks preceding your program.

You may also want to purchase a few iron-on transfers ahead of time and encourage children to wear them on T-shirts at school or in their neighborhoods.

• ***Sing & Play Soundtrack* audiocassette or CD**—Get kids excited about HolyWord Studios! Play HolyWord Studios songs in your Sunday school classes or your other children's ministry programs.

• **Chadder Chipmunk plush puppet**—Invite this furry friend to visit your Sunday school classes—or even to make an appearance during adult worship. Chadder Chipmunk can announce the dates and times for your program. You can even ask Location Leaders to use Chadder to demonstrate HolyWord Studios activities—Chadder playing with an Incredi-Ball...Chadder sampling Movie Munchies...Chadder dancing to "Jesus Loves Me Rock"...the possibilities are as unlimited as your imagination!

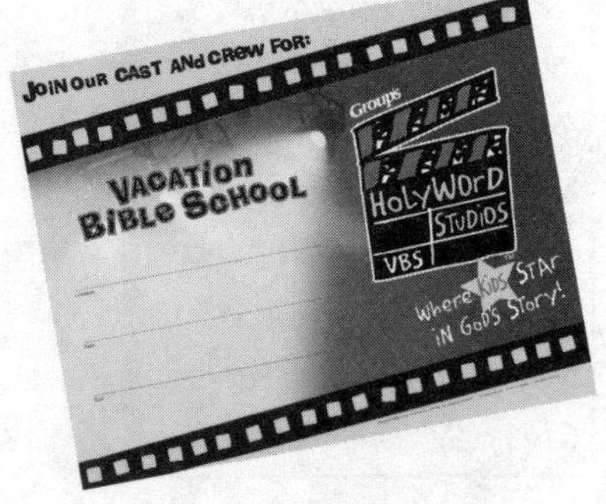

• **HolyWord Studios invitation postcards**—Send personalized invitations to all the families in your church and your community. Just fill in the time, date, and location of your HolyWord Studios program, and drop these postcards in the mail or hand them out at children's ministry events. These colorful postcards are available in packages of fifty.

• **HolyWord Studios posters**—Hang these attractive posters on church or community bulletin boards to publicize your program. Be sure to include the name and phone number of someone to contact for more information.

If you're hanging a poster in your church, surround it with photographs from last year's program. When parents and kids remember the fun they had last year, they'll be eager to come back for even more Bible-learning fun at HolyWord Studios.

• **Giant outdoor theme banner**—Announce HolyWord Studios to your entire neighborhood by hanging this durable, weatherproof banner outside your church. If parents are looking for summer activities for their kids, they'll know right away that your church has a program to meet their needs.

• **HolyWord Studios doorknob danglers**—Hand-deliver information about HolyWord Studios to families in your community with these bright, lively doorknob danglers.

Choose the items you think will work best in your church and community. Then promote your HolyWord Studios program until you're ready to start production!

HolyWord Studios Clip Art

Get ready to star in the greatest story ever told—God's story!

Based on the best-selling book, the Bible! Join us for a week of unforgettable Bible-learning fun at HolyWord Studios!

Studio location:

____
(church name)

The shoot will last:

____
(VBS dates)

All cast members should report at:

____
(VBS starting time)

All cast members released at:

____
(VBS ending time)

For more information, call:

____
(church phone number)

Get ready to star in the greatest story ever told—God's story!

Based on the best-selling book, the Bible! Join us for a week of unforgettable Bible-learning fun at HolyWord Studios!

Studio location:

____
(church name)

The shoot will last:

____
(VBS dates)

All cast members should report at:

____
(VBS starting time)

All cast members released at:

____
(VBS ending time)

For more information, call:

____
(church phone number)

Permission to photocopy this bulletin insert from Group's HolyWord Studios: HolyWord Studios Director Manual granted for local church use. Copyright © Group Publishing, Inc., P.O. Box 481, Loveland, CO 80539.

Dear Parents:

Lights, camera, action! This summer, ______________________________
(name of church)

is letting kids star in God's story at **HolyWord Studios**.

Each day your children will be a part of fun Bible learning they can see...hear...touch...and even taste! Unique craft items, team-building games, lively Bible songs, and healthy treats are just a few of the HolyWord Studios activities that help kids view God's story from a new angle. Children will also enjoy hands-on Bible adventures and daily video visits from Chadder Chipmunk™! Your kids will even participate in a hands-on missions project called Operation Kid-to-Kid™, that involves nearly a million other children across North America!

HolyWord Studios is great fun for children of all ages; even teenagers will enjoy signing on as "Film Crew Leaders" who help younger children. And parents, grandparents, and friends are invited to join us each day at ______________________ (time you've scheduled your Show Time) for Show Time—a daily celebration of God's love you won't want to miss.

So mark ______________________ (dates of your VBS) on your calendar. Filming starts at ____________ (VBS starting time), and will wrap at ____________ (VBS ending time). Call ________________ (church phone number) to register your children for a Bible-learning adventure they'll never forget.

Sincerely,

Your HolyWord Studios Director

News Release

Adapt the information in this news release to fit your church's HolyWord Studios program. Then submit typed, double-spaced copies to your local newspapers, radio stations, and TV stations. You may want to check with them for any other specific requirements regarding news releases.

[Name of Church] Invites Children to Star in Bible Adventures at HolyWord Studios.

"This year our church is using the Bible as a script, as we film God's story," says [your church pastor's name]. "We're on Location at HolyWord Studios, where kids won't find any boring reminders of tedious schoolwork. Our HolyWord Studios program will provide fun, memorable Bible-learning activities for kids of all ages. Each day, kids will sing catchy songs, play teamwork-building games, nibble tasty treats from Movie Munchies, dig into Bible adventures, and create Prop Shop Crafts creations they'll take home and play with all summer long. One day, kids will even be special effects experts who make the story of Pharaoh and the plagues come to life!

"HolyWord Studios is an exciting way for kids to learn that God's story is their story," says [your pastor's name]. "Kids will join nearly a million children in North America and take part in a hands-on mission project that will reach needy children across the globe. We'll conclude each day with a festive Show Time program that gets everyone involved in celebrating what they've learned. Family members and friends are encouraged to join us daily for this special time at [time of Show Time]. We hope HolyWord Studios will help our community realize that the Bible is a script that guides us through life."

HolyWord Studios begins at [VBS starting date] and continues through [VBS ending date]. Cast members will meet at [name of church and church address] each day from [VBS starting time] until [VBS ending time]. For information, call [church phone number].

You Can Be a Star!

Join us on location at HolyWord Studios! You'll enjoy cool crafts and wild games, experience thrilling Bible stories, sample tasty snacks, and hear lively music. Plus, you'll meet lots of new friends!

Studio location:

____
(church name)

The shoot will last:

____
(VBS dates)

All cast members should report at:

____
(VBS starting time)

All cast members released at:

____
(VBS ending time)

For more information, call:

____
(church phone number)

Publicity Skit

Have a few volunteers perform this skit before a worship service, during your announcements, at a midweek program, or during children's church or Sunday school.

Setting:

Your church. (That should be easy!)

Props:

You'll need two directors chairs, a container of popcorn, a paper cup, and an assortment of movie candy.

Thumbs Up!

(Wiskel and Gee-Bert are sitting in the directors chairs. Gee-Bert is holding popcorn, a cup, and other candy in his lap. He eats continually throughout the skit.)

Wiskel: Welcome back to "At the Movies" with Wiskel and Gee-Bert. I'm Dean Wiskel, film critic for the Tuna Flats Tri-Annual Newsletter.

Gee-Bert: And I'm Robby Gee-Bert from the Dinkyville Post. As you'll recall, last week we reviewed that epic fishing movie, "Shark White and the Seven Wharfs." Although Dean gave it a thumbs up, something about the plot seemed fishy to me, and I had to give it a thumbs down.

Wiskel: You didn't like it? I thought you were just shaking a Jujube off your thumb! Oh well, I have to remember that you're the same critic who loved that hokey baseball movie disaster, "The Umpire Strikes Back."

Gee-Bert: Yet another film we disagree on. This week we're turning our attention to the latest production to come from HolyWord Studios. This dynamite film covers the greatest story ever told—God's story. In fact, HolyWord Studios used that best seller, the Bible, as a script for the production.

Wiskel: The plot weaves together the story of baby Moses and God's care for the Israelites, and makes a fantastic connection to God's provision for us today through Jesus. Aside from the plot, I don't know about you, Robby, but I felt that the best part of all was the cast. This is a marvelous, all-star cast of kids from (name of your town).

Gee-Bert: The kids *were* great, but that's partly due to the fact that they actually make those incredible Movie Munchies snacks. I don't think I've seen such tempting food since I reviewed that double feature, "Citizen Candy Cane" and "Chef Side Story."

HolyWord HiNtS

If you can round up a larger cast, you may want to host a quick round of "HolyWord Squares" to publicize your VBS! Have volunteers dress as Bible characters, such as Moses, Miriam, Pharaoh, Joseph of Arimathea, or Paul. Ask questions that relate to each character's Bible "experiences" and allow them to ad lib silly answers (in character, of course!). Your congregation will love it—and they'll all show up at VBS to see the rest of the Bible "cast" in action!

Wiskel: The snacks were good, and we both laughed our way through Now Playing Games and *Chadder's HolyWord Adventure.* I even saw you get a little nervous when you encountered that Egyptian guard during Blockbuster Bible Adventures.

Gee-Bert: Just another excellent use of special effects—the Bible stories simply came alive.

Wiskel: But the way the cast came together for Operation Kid-to-Kid—what a powerful ending. All in all, I'd have to give this a resounding thumbs up. *(Holds up thumb.)*

Gee-Bert: I'm with you. *(Holds up thumb.)* Wow, we haven't agreed on a movie since that medical thriller, "The Wizard of Gauze." This is phenomenal! Two thumbs up! Well, folks, that's all the time we have today. Until next time, save the aisle seats for us!

Registration
Welcoming Your Film Crews

Making an Unforgettable Impression

HolyWord Studios is a fun place for kids to star in God's story. Once kids sample the activities at each Location, they'll want to star with you all week long. But you can start generating excitement and enthusiasm for HolyWord Studios before kids even set foot on Location.

The excitement starts with preregistration. About a month before your scheduled HolyWord Studios program, begin preregistering children in your church. Preregistration is simple: Just make copies of the "HolyWord Studios Registration Form" (p. 154), and have parents fill them out. Or slip HolyWord Studios registration cards into your church bulletins. (These registration cards are available from Group Publishing and your local Christian bookstore.) Save the completed registration forms; you'll use them to assign Film Crews (described on page 141).

To pique kids' (and parents') interest in preregistration, try incorporating some of the following activities:

- **Show the *Sneak Preview* promotional video clip in your church worship service.** This video clip gives everyone in your church a chance to preview HolyWord Studios. It includes glimpses of each HolyWord Studios Location so church members can get a "sneak peak" at all the fun Bible learning that's packed into the HolyWord Studios program.
- **Have kids in your children's ministry programs design their own HolyWord Studios posters.** Distribute large sheets of poster board, and encourage kids to draw posters about their favorite Bible stories, with "movie" titles and quotes from critics. Children might draw things such as David facing Goliath, with the title "My Giant." Or a picture of Jonah in the belly of the fish, entitled "A Fish Story."
- **Have Sunday school classes work together to turn their rooms into Bible-times movie sets.** Provide old tents, sheets, dowels, and other items that children can use to create Bible-times homes. You might even set out carpet roll cores and green butcher paper and allow children to make palm trees. Be sure to provide pictures of Bible-times homes, tents, and wells to give children ideas for ways to decorate. They may want to stuff paper grocery sacks to make blocks, then stack the blocks in a circle to create a round "well." When your "set" is complete, let kids work together to make paper lights and a camera (using a cereal box and a paper cup, painted black.) Place the

HolyWord HINTS

Clever VBS Directors have told numerous success stories of letting middle-schoolers and high-schoolers work on the "set decorating." One Director had a group of fifth- and sixth-graders work on decorations during a lock-in, the week before VBS began. Aside from setting a spectacular stage for VBS, it was a great way to involve older elementary kids and help them become an important part of the program!

HolyWord HINTS

Many churches use preregistration time as a simple fund-raising time. Ask adults to "sponsor" one or more children who will attend VBS. (Post the total number of children you're expecting at VBS so people have an idea of the number of kids you need to sponsor.) The sponsorship fee can be monetary, or it may be a food donation for Movie Munchies. Each time someone sponsors a child, tape a large gold-foil star to the wall near your registration area. Or make a HolyWord Walk of Fame, and have donors trace their hand prints on large paper stars you've placed on the floor. We've heard of churches funding their entire VBS program through these easy donations!

camera and lights around the set.

• **Chart your preregistration with the HolyWord Studios theme poster.** If you ordered the HolyWord Studios theme poster, hang it in a conspicuous location. Each time someone preregisters, place a gold-foil star around the poster. When it's time for HolyWord Studios to begin, you'll have a wonderful wall decoration and a church filled with superstars!

EXTRA IDEA

If you want to start production with extra style and pizazz, consider planning an all-church HolyWord Studios Gala. Decorate your fellowship hall, church lawn, or a nearby park, and set up one or more of the following "Locations."

• Set up a makeup table where kids and adults can have their faces painted like Egyptians. (You may want to put this next to "Costuming," and set up an area where participants can try on Bible-time costumes, Egyptian jewelry, or fancy headwear.) Be sure to have a videographer on hand to capture your "stars" in their finery!

• Provide modeling dough (or plaster of Paris, if you're really brave) and allow "stars" to make their hand prints. Set up your own star-studded sidewalk!

• Set an instant-print camera near a table of "glamour garb," such as feather boas, star-shaped sunglasses, silly hats, and gloves. Let kids and adults get "dolled up" and snap a fun reminder of their "star status."

• Provide several audiocassette recorders, loaded with blank tapes. Place a sign near this area, labeled "Sound Stage." (This is where audio techs create sound effects that enhance the visuals on a movie.) Have kids and adults make noises such as laugh tracks, thunder and rain, a car that won't start, or hum romantic music.

• Provide snack bar staples such as Good & Plenty, Junior Mints, Hot Tamales, Raisinettes, popcorn, and soda. Or set out star-studded fare including sliced star fruit, or bread, cheese, and lunch meat cut into star shapes.

• Have a few volunteers act as *paparazzi,* flashing cameras and wearing Press Passes tucked into their hats. Reporters can ask participants questions, seek interesting quotes, or simply have them pose for glamour shots for the "fans at home."

• Be sure to have at least one person videotaping your Gala. You can use the edited footage for further promotion—this year or in years to come!

The excitement continues as kids arrive at HolyWord Studios. At registration, remember that some families from your community are coming into contact with your church for the first time. You don't want their first impression to be of long, boring registration lines. To make an unforgettable impression, try the following ideas:

• **Prepare a large "Welcome, Cast and Crew!" sign, and post it behind your registration table.** Ask an artistic person in your church to write, "Welcome, Cast and Crew! Production of God's Story Begins Here" in large block letters on a large sheet of poster board or butcher paper. Decorate the sign with paints, markers, glitter, and stars for a dazzling look.

• **Set up the HolyWord Studios Starter Kit can as a display on your registration table.** Set the can on top of a gold or silver foil sheet of wrapping paper for a glamorous feel. You may want to fill the can with Raisinettes, popcorn, or Good & Plenty for kids to enjoy as they register.

• **Play the *Sing & Play Soundtrack* audiocassette or CD.** The fun, upbeat music will provide a festive atmosphere.

• **Use a Chadder Chipmunk puppet (available from Group Publishing and your local Christian bookstore) to greet kids who are waiting in the registration line.** Younger children who might be afraid to leave their parents or caregivers will be reassured by this fuzzy friend—especially when they hear that they'll get to see him each day in the *Chadder's HolyWord Adventure* video. And if you've used Group's VBS in the past, children will delight in seeing Chadder—their familiar, furry friend!

• **Pass out sample Movie Munchies.** You can use a snack from the Movie Munchies Leader Manual or you can come up with your own. Be sure to include drinks—especially if the weather's hot.

Get ready for an all-star adventure!

Setting Up Film Crews

One week before HolyWord Studios begins, assign preregistered kids to Film Crews. Participating in Film Crews is an important part of kids' HolyWord Studios experience, so use care and consideration when making Film Crew assignments. Follow the guidelines given in the planning section of this manual under "One Week Before HolyWord Studios" (p. 51). If you don't know very many of the kids who will attend HolyWord Studios, ask Sunday school teachers or other Christian education workers to help you assign kids to crews.

HolyWord HiNtS

Prayerfully consider the responsibility of setting up Film Crews. These small groups have a powerful impact on children, helping them form special relationships and memories.

Step One: Inventory Your Registrations

• When you're ready to assign crews, make nine copies of the "Age-Level Roster" form (p. 151). Label the forms with grades K, 1, 2, 3, 4, and 5; do the same using "3-year-olds," "4-year-olds," and "5-year-olds" (for 5-year-olds who have not yet attended kindergarten). List the names of preregistered kids on the appropriate age-level rosters.

A Cue From Our Crew

When we used sixth-graders as assistant crew leaders, we learned that, depending on interests and maturity level, some were interested in doing the crafts, games, and snacks as participants rather than being crew leaders. Use your best judgment as each situation arises. Be flexible so you can provide the best possible experience for your "tweenagers."

HolyWord HiNtS

Once you've determined the number of Film Crews you'll have, ask volunteers or HolyWord Studios staff to help create a complete Film Crew bag for each Film Crew. Place a permanent marker, five name badges, five one-yard lengths of lanyard or yarn, five Elementary or Preschool Student Books, and five elementary or preschool HolyWord Studios sticker sheets inside each Film Crew bag. (You'll also need five Bible highlighters in each elementary bag.) You may want to staple a list of the crew members' names to the bag, so they can look and see who will be in their crews. On Day 1, simply give each Film Crew Leader a bag…and they'll be ready for the adventure to begin! Almost all of the above items are available from Group Publishing and your local Christian bookstore.

• Count how many kids have preregistered for your HolyWord Studios, and divide them into two groups: elementary-age children and preschool-age children. Elementary-age children have completed kindergarten, fifth grade, or any grade in between. Be sure to check forms carefully; some families may have registered more than one child on one form. If children who have completed sixth grade want to participate in your program, that's OK; keep in mind, though, that most of the HolyWord Studios activities are designed for slightly younger kids. HolyWord Studios is designed to use young people in grades six and higher in leadership roles; encourage mature sixth-graders to serve as Assistant Film Crew Leaders. For other ideas about how upper-elementary kids can participate in HolyWord Studios, see page 27.

Step Two: Determine How Many Film Crews You'll Have

• Each Film Crew will have no more than five kids and one adult or teenage Film Crew Leader. (Preschool crews may have a high school leader.) Divide the total number of preregistered elementary-age kids by five to discover how many elementary Film Crews you'll have. Do the same with preschool preregistrations. Use the line below to help you determine this.

If you want to encourage kids to bring their friends to HolyWord Studios, you may want to place only three or four kids in each crew. This will allow you to add to your crews.

Once you've determined the number of preschool and elementary crews you'll need, check to see that you've recruited enough Film Crew Leaders. Remember that you'll need a Film Crew Leader for every crew, plus a few extra leaders on hand on Day 1.

Number of (elementary or preschool) kids ________/ at five kids per crew = Number of **Film Crews**________.

Step Three: Assign Film Crews

• Photocopy the "Film Crew Roster" form (p. 152). You'll need one form for every four Film Crews.

• Assign a Film Crew Leader to each Film Crew. It's helpful to indicate whether the leader is an adult (A), a teenager (T), or junior higher (J).

• Preschool Film Crews

Gather the age-level rosters for ages three, four, and five. Beginning with the three-year-old age-level roster, assign one child from each preschool age-level roster to each preschool Film Crew. Since each crew has five spaces, you'll have more than one representative of some age levels in each crew. Remember, it's helpful to have a mixture of preschool ages in each crew so crew leaders can work with three-year-olds, while five-year-olds may be a bit more self-sufficient. Be sure to check off the names on the age-level rosters as you assign them to crews.

• Elementary Film Crews

Gather the elementary age-level rosters. Beginning with the kindergarten age-level roster, assign one child from each age-level roster to each Film Crew. Since each crew has only five spaces, you won't be able to have every age level in every crew. Check off the names on the age-level rosters as you assign them to crews. Refer to the examples below for ways to spread age levels evenly among your Film Crews.

You aren't *required* to group children in combined-age Film Crews, but we strongly recommend it because it works so well. Children, young and old alike, help one another throughout their time together. Plus you'll minimize discipline problems because the diversity frees children from the need to compete with peers of the same age. For more information on the benefits of combining ages, see page 25.

If you have an equal number of children in each grade level,

• fill one-third of your crews with kids who have completed kindergarten and grades two through five.

• fill one-third of your crews with kids who have completed grades one through five.

• fill one-third of your crews with kids who have completed kindergarten through grade four.

If you have an abundance of younger children,

• group kindergartners, second-graders, third-graders, and fifth-graders together. Assign two kindergartners to each crew if necessary. Remind Film Crew Leaders to encourage the fifth-graders to help younger children. Fifth-graders might even be named "Assistant Film Crew Leaders."

• group kids in grades one through four together. Assign two first-graders to each crew if necessary.

If you have an abundance of older children,

• group kindergartners, first-graders, second-graders, and fourth-graders together. Assign two fourth graders to each crew if necessary.

• group grades two through five together. Assign two fifth-graders to each crew if necessary.

If you have fewer than five kids per Film Crew,

• vary the age-level mix, if possible, so you'll have open spaces in your program at every age level. These spaces can be filled by kids who haven't preregistered.

Step Four: Complete the Master List

• Double-check to make sure you've assigned each participant to a Film Crew. Then write kids' Film Crew numbers on their registration forms next to their names.

• Alphabetize the registration forms, and then transfer kids' names and crew numbers to the "Alphabetical Master List" (p. 153). Put a P in the crew-number space next to each preschooler's name.

• Give the preschool registration forms, age-level rosters, and Film Crew rosters to the Preschool Bible Playhouse Director.

Bring the "Age-Level Roster" lists, "Film Crew Roster" lists, and "Alphabetical Master List" with you to registration!

A Cue From Our Crew

Our Film Crew Leaders are always amazed at how well kids work together in a multi-age setting! Most kids truly enjoy being with children of other ages—and your discipline problems will practically disappear! However, if some children insist on being with same-age friends, put pairs of friends in the same Film Crew. This allows children to be with their buddies, while giving them wonderful opportunities to interact with kids of other ages and abilities.

HolyWord HiNtS

It's a good idea to keep gender in mind when assigning children to Film Crews. If at all possible, be sure to include more than one child of each gender. Even though HolyWord Studios activities are designed to help kids work together, kids will feel at ease more quickly if there are a few members of their own gender in the group.

A Cue From Our Crew

We had Film Crew Leaders make their crew posters during the training session (see pp. 105-123). Not only did this save time on the first day of VBS, but it got the crew leaders thinking (and praying) about their crews before VBS had even started. Besides, they did an amazing job and made the posters bright and colorful!

A Cue From Our Crew

We posted the crew posters numerically, so kids could easily find their crew leaders on the first day. Later in the week, crew leaders mentioned that kids sitting in the back rows were feeling a little disconnected from what was happening up front. So, mid-week, we rotated the crew posters so new kids could sit near the front and really tune in to the program. It was a super way to keep everyone in on the action!

HolyWord HiNtS

Having Film Crew Leaders write kids' names on their name badges is a nice way for leaders to learn the names of their crew members. Plus, they can make them all large and legible!

Let Film Crew Leaders Help With Studio Sign-In

Film Crew Leaders can help you breeze through registration! They meet and greet kids and help keep kids busy while others are standing in line. Read on to find out how Film Crew Leaders help make registration a snap.

Film Crew Leader Registration Supplies

Each Film Crew Leader will need the following supplies:

- a permanent marker,
- colorful washable markers or posters,
- one sheet of poster board,
- one Film Crew bag,
- a copy of the "Film Crew Roster" for his or her crew, and
- masking tape.

Each child will need a Student Book, a HolyWord Studios sticker sheet, and a name badge strung on one yard of lanyard or yarn. Give these items to the Film Crew Leaders and have them store the items in their Film Crew bags.

Film Crew Leader Registration Procedures

- Give each Film Crew Leader a Film Crew Leader cap to wear. This helps Location Leaders and kids recognize crew leaders.
- When Film Crew Leaders arrive, they'll write their Film Crew numbers on sheets of poster board then hang the number posters *where they can be seen easily* in the Sing & Play Soundtrack area. It helps if leaders hang the posters in numerical order.
- After children complete the registration process, they'll meet their Film Crew Leaders by their crew-number posters in Sing & Play Soundtrack.
- Film Crew Leaders will greet kids and welcome them to HolyWord Studios. Leaders will use permanent markers to write kids' names and crew numbers on their name badges. If additional kids have been assigned to Film Crews during registration, Film Crew Leaders will update their copies of the "Film Crew Roster."
- Film Crews will work on decorating their crew-number posters while they wait for others to arrive. This is a fun time for Film Crew Leaders and crew members to get acquainted.

Registration Supplies

For registration, you'll need the following supplies:

- entry decorations such as Christmas lights, movie posters, and a red carpet
- three tables
- four signs:
  - ✔ "Preregistered—kindergarten through fifth grade"
  - ✔ "Walk-in registration—kindergarten through fifth grade"
  - ✔ two "Preschool registration" signs with arrows pointing to the Preschool Bible Playhouse
- two copies of each completed elementary "Film Crew Roster" (p. 152)
- one copy of each completed preschool "Film Crew Roster" (p. 152)
- three copies of each completed elementary "Age-Level Roster" (p. 151)
- two copies of each completed preschool "Age-Level Roster" (p. 151)
- two copies of the completed "Alphabetical Master List" (p. 153)
- plenty of pens and pencils
- at least five volunteers, including the Registrar
- chairs for your volunteers
- blank copies of the "HolyWord Studios Registration Form" (p. 154)

HolyWord HiNtS

You may want to give each Film Crew Leader a few extra name badges and one-yard lengths of lanyard or yarn for walk-in registrants who may join their crews.

Registration Setup

Before registration, set up two tables in your church's foyer or entry area. If weather permits, you may want to set up your tables outside to allow more room. (It's a good idea to place these tables far apart to avoid a bottleneck.) Put the "Preregistered—kindergarten through fifth grade" sign above one table. Put the "Walk-in registration—kindergarten through fifth grade" sign above the other table. Set up chairs for your volunteers at each table. Be sure to place your signs high enough for everyone to clearly see!

A Cue From Our Crew

We discovered that it was helpful to tape lists and rosters to the registration tables. That way they didn't blow away or get lost or torn. Plus registration helpers had easy access to all information and could easily scan the lists to find a child's name.

Preregistered Table

On the table below the preregistered sign, place

- a copy of the completed "Alphabetical Master List" (p. 153),
- a copy of each completed "Film Crew Roster" (p. 152), and
- several pencils.

Walk-In Registration Table

On the table below the walk-in registration sign, place

- a copy of each completed elementary "Age-Level Roster" (p. 151),
- a copy of each completed "Film Crew Roster" (p. 152),
- copies of the "Registration Form" (p. 154), and
- several pens or pencils.

Take the Express Lane!

Consider an "Express Preregistered Check-In" system. Have a couple of volunteers stand at the entryway, holding copies of the "Alphabetical Master List." Kids who are preregistered can tell the "Express Checkers" their names and have the Checkers look at the list to see which Film Crews kids are in. Or if you're low on volunteers, enlarge your "Alphabetical Master List," and post several copies of it near your registration area. Kids (and parents) can check the list to find what Film Crews they're on and then simply find their crew numbers and Film Crew Leaders!

Preschool Registration Table

Set up a table (or several if you have more than twenty-five preschoolers) outside your Preschool Bible Playhouse area. Put the two "Preschool registration" signs (with arrows pointing to the Preschool Bible Playhouse) near your main registration area.

On the preschool registration table(s), place

- a copy of each completed preschool "Age-Level Roster" (p. 151),
- a copy of each preschool "Film Crew Roster" (p. 152),
- blank copies of the "Registration Form" (p. 154), and
- several pencils.

Registration: Here They Come!

1. Arrange for your registration workers (including Film Crew Leaders) to arrive at least thirty minutes *before* registration is scheduled to begin.

2. Cut apart the individual "Film Crew Roster" lists from the third set of "Film Crew Roster" lists you copied. As Film Crew Leaders arrive, give each a copy of his or her crew roster.

3. Send elementary Film Crew Leaders to the Sing & Play Soundtrack area and preschool Film Crew Leaders to Preschool Bible Playhouse. Explain that as kids arrive, they'll find their Film Crew numbers at the registration tables and then join their crew leaders and other Film Crew members in Sing & Play Soundtrack or Preschool Bible Playhouse.

4. Assign two workers to the preregistration table, two workers to the walk-in table, and at least one worker to the preschool table.

5. Go over the registration instructions for each area (preregistered, walk-in registration, and preschool). Answer any questions workers have, and offer the following helpful hints:

- Kindly insist that each participant fill out a complete registration form, including all pertinent health and emergency information. *This is very important!*
- If families have both preschool and elementary children, encourage them to go to the preschool area first. This will keep preschoolers from getting fidgety as they wait for their parents to register their older siblings.
- Walk-in registration will naturally take more time. As families are filling out their registration forms, scan the Film Crew rosters for openings. This will help you complete Film Crew assignments quickly.

After you've answered all the questions, have registration workers and Film Crew Leaders take their places. You're ready to welcome kids to HolyWord Studios!

Important!

It's important that you know at all times who is in each Film Crew. In an emergency or if a parent needs to pick up a child midprogram, you'll want an accurate "map" of where everyone is.

HolyWord HINTS

It's important that you have a completed registration form for *each child,* not just one for each family! When families place all their children on one form, it can be difficult to find information that's specific to each child.

After Registration

> **A Cue From Our Crew**
> *It really is important to touch base with Film Crew Leaders after the first day (or even after each day!). We made a few "tweaks" in Film Crews, such as pairing up a less-experienced crew leader with a veteran leader. By catching problems or miscommunications early on, everyone enjoyed a smoother program!*

After registration on Day 1, shout out a loud, "Take Five!" Your biggest job is done! Read on to find out how you can ensure that Days 2 through 5 are successful.

• **Leave your registration tables in place.** You'll want to continue welcoming children as they arrive on Days 2 through 5, as well as registering any newcomers. Tape the "Alphabetical Master List" to the table, and set out several pencils or pens. To chart attendance, let children (or parents) check each day's box as they come to HolyWord Studios.

• **Check in with Location Leaders and Film Crew Leaders.** Even if you've "wrapped" the details ahead of time, unforeseen glitches can mar your production. After you've gone through one day's activities, meet with your cast to evaluate how things went. Location Leaders may find that they need additional supplies or alternative room assignments. Inexperienced Film Crew Leaders may be having trouble handling unruly children in their Film Crews. If this is the case, you may need to reassign some children to different crews or rearrange your groups so that Film Crews with inexperienced leaders visit Locations with crews that have experienced leaders.

• **Update your "Alphabetical Master List" and "Film Crew Rosters" as needed.** Be sure to check with the volunteers at the walk-in table. Kids who completed walk-in registration on Day 1 can be added to the "Alphabetical Master List" for speedier check-in through the rest of the week. If you've rearranged your Film Crews, make sure each Film Crew receives an updated "Film Crew Roster."

You did it! Now sit back, take five, and enjoy the feature presentation!

> **A Cue From Our Crew**
> *Through our field tests and from customer feedback, we've learned (oftentimes, the hard way) that two-year-olds really are too young for a program like this. Kindly insist that only three-year-olds may join the program—everyone (especially those little ones) will appreciate your efforts in the long run!*

HolyWord Studios Registration Instructions

Photocopy these instructions, and place copies in all registration areas. Have registration workers highlight their areas of responsibility.

Preschool: Preregistered and Walk-In

Preschool registration will take place ____________________.

1. Greet family members or caregivers with a warm smile. Thank them for bringing the children to HolyWord Studios.
2. Ask for each child's name and age (three, four, or five years old). Greet each child by name, and thank him or her for coming.

If a child has completed kindergarten or is older than six, send the family to the elementary preregistered line.

3. Have parents or caregivers complete registration forms for unregistered children.
4. Locate each registered child's name on the "Alphabetical Master List," and place a check mark on the Day 1 box to indicate that he or she is present.
5. If a child is a walk-in, scan the preschool "Film Crew Roster" lists to find an appropriate Film Crew to place him or her in. Add the child's name to the "Film Crew Roster" list as well as to the "Alphabetical Master List."
6. Point out the child's Film Crew Leader, and have a Preschool Bible Playhouse volunteer guide the child to the Film Crew Leader.
7. Tell the family members or caregivers what time they can pick up their preschoolers in the Show Time area each day. Assure them that an adult or teenage Film Crew Leader will stay with children until the family members or caregivers arrive.

Elementary: Preregistered

Elementary registration will take place ____________________.

1. Greet family members or caregivers with a warm smile. Thank them for bringing the children to HolyWord Studios.
2. Ask for each child's name and the grade he or she last completed (kindergarten through fifth grade). Greet each child by name, and thank him or her for coming.

If a child has not yet attended kindergarten, send the family to Preschool Bible Playhouse for registration.

3. Locate each child's name on the "Alphabetical Master List" or, if a child's name isn't on the list, send the family to the walk-in table to complete a new registration form.
4. Put a check mark by each child's name to indicate that he or she is present at HolyWord Studios. Then tell the child his or her Film Crew number and crew leader's name.
5. Direct children to the Sing & Play Soundtrack area, and explain that crew leaders are waiting there with name badges. Tell children to look for the large signs with their crew numbers on them.
6. Tell the family members or caregivers what time they can pick up their children each day. Encourage them to come early and participate in Show Time.

HolyWord Studios Registration Instructions

Elementary: Walk-In Registration

Elementary registration will take place ______________________________.

1. Greet family members or caregivers with a warm smile. Thank them for bringing the children to HolyWord Studios.
2. Ask for each child's name and the grade he or she last completed (kindergarten through fifth grade). Greet each child by name, and thank him or her for coming.

If a child has not yet attended kindergarten, send the family to Preschool Bible Playhouse for registration.

3. Add each child's name to the appropriate "Age-Level Roster." Have the child's parent or caregiver complete a registration form.
4. While parents fill out registration forms, assign each child to a Film Crew. Refer to the "Film Crew Rosters" to see which crews have openings. Look for a Film Crew *without* a member in that child's grade. *If you have questions about assigning children to Film Crews, see your Studio Director!*
5. Write each child's Film Crew number on his or her completed registration form. (Later you'll need to add the new name and Film Crew assignment to the "Alphabetical Master List.")
6. Direct children to the Sing & Play Soundtrack area, and explain that crew leaders are waiting there with name badges. Tell children to look for the large signs with their crew numbers on them.
7. Tell the family members or caregivers what time they can pick up their children each day. Encourage them to come early and participate in Show Time.

Age-Level Roster

Grade: ____________

Film Crew Roster

Film Crew Number: ____________________

Film Crew Leader: ____________________

Film Crew Members

1. ____________________
2. ____________________
3. ____________________
4. ____________________
5. ____________________

Film Crew Number: ____________________

Film Crew Leader: ____________________

Film Crew Members

1. ____________________
2. ____________________
3. ____________________
4. ____________________
5. ____________________

Film Crew Number: ____________________

Film Crew Leader: ____________________

Film Crew Members

1. ____________________
2. ____________________
3. ____________________
4. ____________________
5. ____________________

Film Crew Number: ____________________

Film Crew Leader: ____________________

Film Crew Members

1. ____________________
2. ____________________
3. ____________________
4. ____________________
5. ____________________

Alphabetical Master List

Name	Film Crew Number	Day 1	Day 2	Day 3	Day 4	Day 5
		❑	❑	❑	❑	❑
		❑	❑	❑	❑	❑
		❑	❑	❑	❑	❑
		❑	❑	❑	❑	❑
		❑	❑	❑	❑	❑
		❑	❑	❑	❑	❑
		❑	❑	❑	❑	❑
		❑	❑	❑	❑	❑
		❑	❑	❑	❑	❑
		❑	❑	❑	❑	❑
		❑	❑	❑	❑	❑
		❑	❑	❑	❑	❑
		❑	❑	❑	❑	❑
		❑	❑	❑	❑	❑
		❑	❑	❑	❑	❑
		❑	❑	❑	❑	❑
		❑	❑	❑	❑	❑
		❑	❑	❑	❑	❑
		❑	❑	❑	❑	❑

HolyWord Studios Registration Form

(one per child)

Name: ______________________________

Street address: ______________________________

City: ____________________ State: __________ ZIP: __________

Home telephone: (________) ____________________ Age: __________

Last school grade completed: ______________________________

In case of emergency, contact: ______________________________

Mother: ______________________________

Father: ______________________________

Other: ______________________________

Allergies or other medical conditions: ______________________________

Home church: ______________________________

Film Crew number (for church use only): ______________________________

HolyWord Hints
Pointers for a Powerful Production!

Daily Staff Devotions

Plan to meet with your Location Leaders and Film Crew Leaders for fifteen to twenty minutes before your program begins each day. Use this time to give announcements, address questions or concerns, and pray together. Ministering to children is rewarding but hard work, so you may also want to refresh your staff daily with an encouraging devotional. The following devotions tie into the HolyWord Studios daily Bible Points, and help your cast understand the importance of these Points in the lives of children.

HolyWord HiNtS

Due to last-minute details, it can be tough to set aside time to meet *before* VBS. You may want to use these devotions after each day's program, as a reflection and encouragement to your staff.

Day 1

Handle With Care

The Point:

God cares for us.

The Point

Form a circle and hold a bottle of bubble solution. Say: **Today at HolyWord Studios, you'll begin an important, caring relationship with a special group of kids. Let's practice caring for a bubble to get you ready for caring for the kids at HolyWord Studios.**

Blow a bubble, and catch it on the bubble wand. Pass the wand (and bubble) around the circle. If the bubble pops, allow the person who popped the bubble to blow a new one. When the bubble wand comes back to you, pop the bubble and put the wand away. Ask:

- **What was tricky about passing the bubble?**
- **How did you see people moving to keep the bubble from popping?**

HolyWord HiNtS

This might be a good time to use the mini-bubbles (that kids will receive on Friday as a surprise ending). Not only are these wonderful bubbles easy to use, but this activity will be a great way to tie everything together for your staff.

Say: **Just as any rough movements might have burst the bubble, our thoughtless actions and words can quickly "burst" the joy in the little ones we'll serve. Today we're learning that God cares for us.** Form pairs or trios, and have groups discuss the following questions. Ask:

The Point

- **How was moving the bubble like caring for kids?**
- **Why do you think it's important for kids to understand that God cares for them?**

Have groups share their responses, then say: **God cares for us. God cares for**

The Point

our physical needs, as well as our emotional needs. Ask:

• **What kinds of needs do the kids at our VBS have?**

Say: **God knows the needs of these children, even before they tell him. Listen to Matthew 6:8b.** Read aloud Matthew 6:8b, then ask:

The Point

• **What does this passage say about how God cares for us?**

• **How does this passage describe God?**

• **What are some specific ways you can care for the kids at VBS this week?**

HolyWord HINTS

Staff devotions are a super time to show your staff the effectiveness of pair-shares!

Pass the bubble solution and wand around the circle. This time, let each staff member blow a bubble and silently pray for the children that he or she will interact with during VBS. Close by praying: **Caring Father, we are so glad that you care for every part of our lives. Help us be caring and loving to the children at VBS this week. Guide us as we show them your heart. In Jesus' name, amen.**

Day 2

Safe in God's Hands

The Point:

The Point

God protects us.

Set up a simple obstacle course in your meeting area. You might scatter chairs around the room, overturn a table, or toss a handful of blocks on the floor. Have staff members form pairs and stand at one end of the room. Say: **First, decide which partner will be the actor (or actress) and who will be the director.** Pause while partners determine their roles. **Sometimes, actors and actresses have to perform tricky stunts. In this activity, the performers will close their eyes while the directors guide them through the room, trying to avoid these "hazards." Directors, you may guide your performer any way you choose—verbally or physically.**

While pairs are crossing the room, play "I Walk by Faith" from the *Sing & Play Soundtrack* audiocassette or CD. After partners have made it across the room, have them switch roles and move across to the other side of the room. Then turn off the cassette or CD, gather in a circle, and ask:

• **What was it like to be the actor or actress?**

• **How did your director guide you?**

• **What feelings did this activity bring up?**

The Point

Say: **Today at HolyWord Studios, kids will discover that God protects us.** Ask:

• **How did your director protect you?**

• **How is that like or unlike God's protection?**

Say: **Today we'll discover that God protected the Israelites and gave them rest—from their hard labor, from their fears, and from the plagues. Let me read a Scripture passage that tells us more about God's protection. As I read this, think about the children at HolyWord Studios.** Read aloud Matthew 11:28, then ask:

• **Why do the kids at VBS need to know this about God?**

• **What burdens do the kids at VBS carry?**

• **How might they live differently, understanding that God protects them?**

Say: **Our obstacle course was harmless and fun, but the real world holds many dangers and burdens for kids today. That's why it's so important that they understand that God will protect them. Even though God doesn't always protect us physically, God does protect us spiritually. That means that sometimes, instead of protecting our bodies, God protects our hearts, giving us peace and rest in him.**

Close by having each person say one or two words that represent something children need protection from. Participants might say words like, "pain," "injury," or "broken hearts." Then close by thanking God that he is mightier than all of those things.

Day 3

God's Love

The Point:

God loves us.

Say: **Well, you've made it halfway through this HolyWord Studios production! Turn to someone near you and describe one "movie clip" or memory that was particularly meaningful from the week.** Allow a moment for pairs to share, then call on a few individuals to share their "clips" from the week.

Say: **Each of you is doing an all-star job in your roles! Keep up the good work!** Hold up a container of bubbles and continue: **I'm sure you're probably ready to let off a little steam, so we'll use these bubbles to give you the opportunity. In this activity, you'll blow several bubbles, then quickly hand the container to another person. Then it's your job to keep your bubbles from popping or hitting the floor. Ready?** Hand the bubble solution to someone nearby, then turn on "Jesus Loves Me Rock" (from the *Sing & Play Soundtrack* audiocassette or CD) while

The Point

A Cue From Our Crew

When we met for lunch each day, we discovered that sharing VBS stories and insights together was meaningful to our staff. It reminded them that they were doing so much more than volunteering—they were truly touching precious lives!

cast members blow their bubbles. When the song is over, allow everyone to pop the bubbles. Then gather together and ask:

• How did you feel during this activity?

• How did you feel when one of your bubbles popped or was lost in the crowd?

The Point

Say: **Today we're learning the important message that God loves us. Matthew 18:14 tells us more about Gods tremendous love.** Read aloud Matthew 18:14, then ask:

• What does this tell us about God's love?

• How does this passage remind you of our game?

• How is God's love different from the attention you gave your bubbles?

Say: **When the Israelites were fleeing Egypt, God made sure that every person made it across the Red Sea. He loved his people so much that he didn't want any one of them to be left behind—and there were more than two million! God loves the children here at HolyWord Studios, too. Each one is precious to him.** Ask:

• How can you show God's love to the kids at VBS today?

Say: **God can use you to shepherd his little ones. A smile, a hug, or an encouraging word may be all that a child needs to see God's love.**

Day 4

A Way

The Point:

The Point

God saves us.

Before this devotion, set a bag of candy or vase of fresh flowers on a table at one end of the room. Have staff members line up at the other end of the room. Say: **This candy is a free gift to anyone who can get to it by following my one rule. No part of your body can touch the floor.** Allow a minute or two for your staff to work together and try to solve the dilemma. While they're talking, walk around in the open space between them and the gift. (This is a subtle hint at the solution.) If participants are still stumped, say: **By the way, did I mention that it's OK for *my* body to touch the floor?** You may need to offer to carry one of the lighter staff members across the room to retrieve the gift. Then gather everyone together. Ask:

• What did you think when I first told you the rules?

Say: **I wanted you to have the gift, so I provided a way for you to get there. It took some sacrifice on my part, but it was worth it to see your**

smiles! Form pairs or trios, and have them discuss the following questions:

- **How does this activity remind you of God's love for us?**
- **Why do you think God provided a way for us to be with him?**
- **How did God save us?**

Let groups share their responses, then say: **Today children will discover that God saves us. Just as the Israelites needed a Passover lamb to escape death, we need Jesus to escape eternal separation from God. Without Jesus, there was no way to God. So God provided Jesus. In fact, that was the whole reason for Jesus' birth!** Read aloud Matthew 1:21.

The Point

Say: **There are children at our VBS who don't know about Jesus. They don't know that there's only one way to God. They don't understand that God has provided a way for them to live in heaven forever. We can be the link that connects them with Jesus, their Savior.**

Have participants link arms and form a circle. Pray: **Gracious Lord, thank you for sending Jesus to save us from our sins. Thank you that he is the Passover lamb to give us new life. We pray for all the children here at Holy-Word Studios who don't know you. Give us the words to say that will help them understand their need for you. Amen.**

HolyWord HINTS

On Day 4, children will hear the message of Jesus' death and resurrection. Since this may be a natural time for children to ask questions about salvation, you may want to photocopy and distribute the "Helping Children Follow Jesus" section (p. 175) to each staff member.

Day 5

Soothing Spirit

The Point:

God is always with us.

The Point

Say: **When my hands feel dry, nothing feels as nice as some soothing lotion. Here, why don't you try some, too?** Pass around a bottle of lightly scented lotion, and let each person put some on his or her hands and rub it in. Then ask:

- **How do your hands feel?**
- **How does lotion help your hands?**
- **How can you tell that you have lotion on your hands?**

Say: **This is a little like the Holy Spirit in our lives. We can't see the Holy Spirit, but we can tell he's working. Just as the lotion soothes, heals, and protects, God's Spirit is a comforter and helper in our lives. There's a well-known passage in Matthew—a powerful promise from God.** Read aloud Matthew 28:19-20.

- **Why do you think God gave his Holy Spirit?**
- **When is a time that you've needed God's Spirit?**

Say: **God promised his Spirit because he knew the challenges we would face as we told others about God. Today we're learning that God is always with us. It's important that kids understand that God wasn't here just this week—God is with them "to the very end of the age"!** Form pairs or trios and have them discuss the following questions:

The Point

- **How can you help kids understand that God will never leave them?**
- **What challenges do kids face? How can God's Spirit help them through those challenges?**

HolyWord HiNtS

You may want to give each staff member a trial-size bottle of sweet-smelling lotion as a thank you and as a reminder of today's devotion.

Allow groups to share their responses, then say: **Just as the lotion can turn dry, chapped hands into soft and smooth ones, God's Spirit can turn dry, hardened hearts into soft and caring ones. And as the lotion soothed your hands, the Holy Spirit can soothe and comfort us when life is difficult.**

Pray and thank God for sending his Holy Spirit. You may want to have pairs or trios spend time praying specifically for the kids they've interacted with this week. Encourage leaders to continually pray for their crew members in the coming weeks, asking God to help children remember that they are an important part of God's story.

Creating a "Reel" HolyWord Studios Production

More than any VBS theme you'll ever have, this theme lends itself wonderfully to video...and the possibilities are endless! Here are some simple tips for creating a "reel" HolyWord Studios production for your church.

- Check out the overview chart on page 10 and use the [camera icon] to guide you in your "shooting schedule." The [camera icon] is a signal that these are great visual activities that will look especially good on "the big screen."
- Have a videographer visit every Location each day. If at all possible, have a few video crews on hand—or act as a one-person crew yourself! (It's easy, and gives you a good excuse to get a sneak peek at all the action!) Get close-ups of kids' reactions to Chadder, interview kids as they work on Prop Shop Crafts, record the giggles and squeals at Now Playing Games, and be sure to capture kids worshipping in Sing & Play Soundtrack.
- While kids are between Locations, get "on-the-spot" interviews. Ask kids what they're learning today; what they like about their Film Crews; what they've liked the best so far; or have them give their best impersonation of Chadder, Carmine, or Hoppy!

Now that you have all this awesome footage, what do you do with it? Here are a few suggestions:

• Have each day's video segment rolling as kids enter Show Time. (Or show the previous day's footage at Sing & Play Soundtrack the next day.) Kids love seeing themselves on the big screen and will be delighted to see what others have said and done. This is a super way to truly make everyone a star!

• Compile your video footage, edit it for time (and clarity), and show it at the last day's Show Time. Since this is the Show Time that most parents will attend, you'll have an automatic way to "recap" the week and show terrific highlights of your VBS week.

• Compile your video footage and show it at the next week's adult worship service. This is a great way to fill everyone in on the fun you had at HolyWord Studios, and it will encourage others to participate in future programs!

• Get duplicates of your production and sell them or give them away as souvenirs. Kids will love this keepsake—and so will parents and grandparents! What an excellent way to follow up with kids who don't attend your church!

You have all the basic HolyWord Studios materials in your Starter Kit. If you want to add sparkle and pizazz to your program, check out some of the following items.

Location Leader Resources

• **Hand clappers**—You and your Location Leaders will keep kids' attention the easy way with these fun and noisy "clappers." Children love a round of applause and will easily hear it in a crowded room or on a playing field. As Studio Director, you'll use the hand clappers to let Film Crews know when it's time to "scout for" their next Locations. Encourage Location Leaders to use the hand clappers any time they need to get kids' attention.

• **HolyWord Studios staff T-shirts**—Outfit your Location Leaders and other helpers in style. These shirts are cool, eye-catching additions to your décor. Kids and adults will love them, and they'll wear them even after HolyWord Studios is over.

• ***Sing & Play Soundtrack* audiocassette or *Sing & Play Soundtrack Music & Clip Art CD***—Reinforce Bible learning by providing each Location Leader with his or her own *Sing & Play Soundtrack* audiocassette or CD. Kids can hum along as they work in Prop Shop Crafts, play Now Playing Games, and enjoy Movie Munchies. You can also offer this audiocassette or CD to families to reinforce Bible learning at home.

A Cue From Our Crew

The color and style of the T-shirts made them appealing to the middle-schoolers and high-schoolers who acted as our "production assistants." Be sure to order plenty, since these older kids will be clamoring for them!

HolyWord HiNtS

We've heard from many churches that purchase cassettes about a month ahead of time, then use the songs in other children's ministry programs. This gives kids a chance to become more familiar with the songs and motions long before your cameras roll! (Remember, the more you order, the cheaper they become!)

HolyWord HiNtS

To make your photo frames extra special, affix a magnetic strip to the back of the frame. (For extra ease, use magnetic strips that have adhesive on one side.) Children can hang the pictures on their refrigerator doors for a constant reminder of VBS fun!

A Cue From Our Crew

"My child hasn't stopped singing those HolyWord Studios songs!" We hear this so often, and—we admit—we smile every time! It's great to know that kids are singing phrases such as "We believe in God, and we all need Jesus" or "Trust in the Lord with all your heart." That's why we believe it's so important to get these resources into homes everywhere.

• ***Sing & Play Soundtrack Transparencies***—Project song lyrics onto a large screen to make it even easier for kids (and adults) to follow along.

• **Movie Munchies chef hat**—Tall, starched, and white, this classic paper chef hat helps your Movie Munchies Leader look the part! Order one for your Movie Munchies Leader, or order several so kids can join in the food-preparation fun.

• ***Preschool Bible Playhouse* audiocassette**—Provide upbeat music for your youngest stars. This cassette includes the HolyWord Studios theme song, "God's Story," as well as other special songs and stories just for preschoolers.

Additional HolyWord Studios Resources

• **HolyWord Studios iron-on transfers**—These colorful transfers allow adults and children to create wearable mementos of their studio experience.

• **HolyWord Studios photo frames**—Help kids remember their starring roles at HolyWord Studios. These sturdy 4x6-inch cardboard frames feature the HolyWord Studios logo and provide plenty of room for you to add your church's name and address. Insert inexpensive photos you've shot during your program, and offer them for sale—or give them to children as special gifts they'll treasure all summer!

• **Chadder Chipmunk puppet**—Preschoolers will love having Chadder visit their room. The Preschool Bible Playhouse Director Manual suggests ways to make this furry friend part of your HolyWord Studios program. You can give Chadder puppets to volunteers to thank them for their help or you can use Chadder puppets to reinforce Bible learning at other children's ministry events.

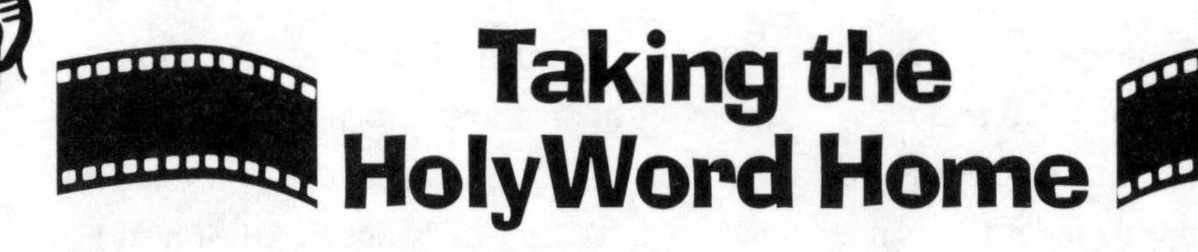

Why Are Family Resources So Important?

Your HolyWord Studios will reach a variety of children from countless backgrounds. Each of these children (and their families) can benefit from having HolyWord Studios resources at home. Not only do the following family resources remind kids of HolyWord Studios fun, but they also provide excellent Bible reinforcement for months after your program has ended. A *Sing & Play Soundtrack* audiocassette may be the only Christian music heard in some children's homes.

What Are Family Resources?

On page 167 of this Director Manual, you'll find an order form that lists five family resources that reinforce Bible learning. From our field tests, we know that kids love items such as the *Sing & Play Soundtrack* audiocassette and CD and *Chadder's HolyWord Adventure* videotape. In fact, several parents arrived early on Day 5 so they could be sure to purchase the limited number of cassettes we had!

Kids love to have mementos of their time at HolyWord Studios. Items such as Chadder plush puppets, HolyWord Studios T-shirts, and iron-on transfers are great reminders of your program.

STUDENT ORDER FORM

Name
Address
City State ZIP
Phone

Complete this order form and return it to your **VBS director**. Or inquire at your local Christian bookstore for these great *HolyWord Studios* items!

How many	Title	Item no.	Price	Total cost
	1. Sing & Play Soundtrack audiocassette	#646847-10054	$10.99	
	2. Sing & Play Soundtrack Music & Clip Art CD	#646847-10152	$16.99	
	3. Sing & Play Soundtrack Music Video	#646847-10053	$24.99	
	4. Chadder's HolyWord Adventure video	#646847-10043	$19.99	
	5. Chadder puppet	#9056	$35.99	

Subtotal $
Shipping & Handling $
Sales tax (CA 7.25%, CO 3%, GA 4%, IA 5%, OH 5%) $
TOTAL $

You can also mail this completed order form and payment to:
Group Publishing, Inc., P.O. Box 485, Loveland, CO 80539
Please add shipping and handling from the chart below.

Shipping & Handling

Order Subtotal	Shipping & Handling
Up to $12	$3.50
$12.01-$20.00	$4.90
$20.01-$50.00	$5.90
$50.01-$75.00	$7.90
$75.01-$100.00	$11.90
$100.01-$150.00	$15.90
$150.01-$200.00	$19.90
$200.01+	$24.90

Permission to photocopy this form from Group's HolyWord Studios: HolyWord Studios Director Manual granted for local church use. Copyright © Group Publishing, Inc., P.O. Box 481, Loveland, CO 80539.

167

How Can Families Get These Resources?

We realize you're busy; after all, you've just directed a VBS program! So we've made it simple to get these important items into the hands of the kids in your program. On page 167, you'll find an order form for five family resources. Now you have three options:

Option 1: Individual Orders

Distribute the order form at the end of Sing & Play Soundtrack on Day 5. Let kids know that they can order the Sing & Play Soundtrack music, Chadder videos, and other fun stuff simply by taking the order form to their local Christian bookstore. Then send the forms home, and let kids and their families act from there.

Option 2: One Church Order

Distribute the order form at the end of Sing & Play Soundtrack on Day 5. Let kids know that they can order the Sing & Play Soundtrack music, Chadder videos, and other fun stuff by having a parent help them fill out the order form. Tell kids they'll then need to bring their money and order form (in an envelope) to you by a specified date. You'll probably want to put the date in your church bulletin the following Sunday.

After the due date, tally the total number of each item, and fill it in on a blank order form or a photocopy of the form on page 167 of this manual. Be sure to keep the original order forms so you can distribute items accurately! Take the master order form to your local Christian bookstore, and purchase the items. The next Sunday, set up a table to distribute HolyWord Studios materials.

Option 3: Back Lot Bazaar

Make it extra easy for families to take home VBS fun, by setting up a Studio Store! Use the order form to order items a few weeks before your HolyWord Studios begins. (Check out the following box to help determine quantities.) Then set a price for each

HolyWord HINTS

"Selling things at church? That seems so commercial!" We've heard this cry before, but experience has shown that providing these quality, kid-friendly resources is an excellent way to reinforce Bible learning at home. When kids listen to Sing & Play Soundtrack songs, they're reminded of God's amazing story. Each time kids look at their studio photos, they'll be reminded of the fun they had exploring God's Word. And kids can even use *Chadder's HolyWord Adventure* video to share the good news of Jesus with their friends! It works!

A Cue From Our Crew

In all of our field test experience, we've found that families really wanted to purchase mementos of a spectacular, meaningful week. You'll be amazed at the overwhelming response when you make these items available.

item. Decide how much money you'll earn on each item you sell. Remember—any money you make can go to your church's missions, children's ministry program, or to local community outreach programs.

Then set up shop! Place the items on a table, just outside the Show Time area. Staff your Studio Store with a few willing volunteers (or youth group members) and open your "doors" after Show Time ends. You'll be amazed at the overwhelming response!

Recommended Advance Order Quantities

Item	Quantity
Chadder's HolyWord Adventure video	10 percent of VBS enrollment
Sing & Play Soundtrack audiocassette	20 percent of VBS enrollment
Sing & Play Soundtrack Music Video	5 percent of VBS enrollment
Chadder plush puppet	5 percent of VBS enrollment
HolyWord photo frame	75 percent of VBS enrollment

It's that easy!

STUDENT ORDER FORM

Name ______________________________

Address ______________________________

____

City ______________ State ________ ZIP ___________

Phone ______________________________

Complete this order form and return it to your **VBS director.** Or inquire at your local Christian bookstore for these great *HolyWord Studios* items!

HOW MANY	TITLE	ITEM NO.	PRICE	TOTAL COST
	1. *Sing & Play Soundtrack* audiocassette	#646847-10054	$10.99	
	2. *Sing & Play Soundtrack Music & Clip Art CD*	#646847-10152	$16.99	
	3. *Sing & Play Soundtrack Music Video*	#646847-10053	$24.99	
	4. *Chadder's HolyWord Adventure* video	#646847-10043	$19.99	
	5. Chadder puppet	#9056	$35.99	

Subtotal $ ___________

Shipping & Handling $ ___________

Sales tax (CA 7.25%, CO 3%, GA 4%, IA 5%, OH 5%) $ ___________

TOTAL $ ___________

You can also mail this completed order form and payment to:
Group Publishing, Inc., P.O. Box 485, Loveland, CO 80539

PLEASE ADD SHIPPING AND HANDLING FROM THE CHART BELOW.

Shipping & Handling

ORDER SUBTOTAL	SHIPPING & HANDLING
Up to $12	$3.50
$12.01-$20.00	$4.90
$20.01-$50.00	$5.90
$50.01-$75.00	$7.90
$75.01-$100.00	$11.90
$100.01-$150.00	$15.90
$150.01-$200.00	$19.90
$200.01+	$24.90

Health and Safety Concerns

Each Location leader manual gives safety tips for specific Location activities. As Studio Director, however, you're responsible for larger health and safety concerns that may affect the entire VBS. The information below may alert you to health and safety concerns that require your attention.

Health Issues

You'll want to maintain a first-aid kit in a central location. Stock your first-aid kit with adhesive bandages of different sizes, first-aid cream, antibacterial ointment, sterile gauze pads, and insect repellent. You may also want to provide a place for children to lie down if they feel ill. Keep children's registration forms near your first-aid area so you can call parents or caregivers in case of serious injury.

Your HolyWord Studios registration form provides a spot for parents or caregivers to identify food allergies. Dairy allergies are common, but you may also have children who are allergic to gluten (wheat, rye, barley, or oats); nuts; or other foods.

Most of the snacks suggested in the Movie Munchies Leader Manual will require only slight modifications for children with food allergies. Consult with the Movie Munchies Leader about modifying snacks or about substituting flavored rice cakes, popcorn, fruits, or raw vegetables to accommodate children with food allergies.

Insurance: Make Sure You're Covered

Your church probably already has an insurance policy or policies that are intended to protect you from loss as a result of fire, theft, injury, or lawsuits. Your program is probably covered by your regular insurance, but you should double-check with your insurance agent to be sure. You're not likely to have serious injuries, but you'll want to be prepared just in case.

Facilities: Keeping Your Studio Back Lot Beautiful

Many accidents can be prevented by well-maintained facilities. After you've selected Location meeting areas, check each area for potential hazards. Remove broken or dangerous items, and be sure to lock storage areas that contain chemicals, cleaning solutions, or other toxic materials.

Your church is about to become a high-traffic area! Keep in mind that you'll probably need to clean bathrooms and empty trash daily. You'll also want to spot-check hallways, lobbies, and meeting rooms for trash, stray Film Crew bags, and lost-and-found items.

Child Abuse: Keeping Kids Safe

Child abuse can take many forms. While you may feel sure that no one in your church would physically or sexually abuse a child in your program, emotional abuse or neglect can be harder to detect. Prevent child abuse by enlisting only staff members that you know and trust and by discussing your concerns and expectations with them ahead of time.

HolyWord Studios field test directors reported few or no discipline problems. But you'll want to talk with your staff about how you'll handle any that do arise. Discuss appropriate and inappropriate staff responses to situations that require discipline. Photocopy and distribute the "What's a Film Crew Leader?" handout from page 118 of this manual. This handout suggests positive-language responses for easy classroom management. Remind staff members that you expect them to model God's love in all they say and do.

HolyWord Studios activities are designed so that children are always supervised by a Location Leader and several Film Crew Leaders. You may want to point this out to parents who are concerned about adequate supervision. To avoid even the appearance of impropriety, encourage each staff member to avoid spending time alone with a child. Suggest that staff members escort children in pairs or small groups for bathroom and drinking fountain stops. A good rule for safe touching is to never touch a child where his or her bathing suit would cover.

Use these health and safety tips to set up a HolyWord Studios program that ensures the physical, emotional, and spiritual well-being of everyone involved.

HolyWord HINTS

Some churches require volunteers to go through a short class, seminar, or workshop on appropriate actions when working with children. This is an excellent idea, especially if less-experienced teenagers and adults will be helping out. Check with your church leaders to see if they know of (or have led) a class that would be helpful to you.

Kids With Special Needs

Physical Disabilities

If you know you'll have physically challenged children at your program, you'll need to make sure your Location areas are wheelchair accessible. You may also want to recruit a staff member to look out for these children. This staff member can ask parents or caretakers about specific needs such as

- whether kids have special equipment such as wheelchairs,
- what kids can and cannot eat,
- what kids need help doing,
- what kids like to do for themselves, and
- what kids enjoy most.

Because children work together and help each other in Film Crews, most physically challenged children will get the help they need from their crew members and Film Crew Leaders. However, if a physically challenged child needs constant help to participate in Location activities, consider assigning an additional Film Crew Leader to his or her crew. For this position, choose someone who will be sensitive and who is capable of responding to the child's needs.

Physically challenged children may be shy, but often they're very bright and innovative. Film Crew Leaders can encourage them to shine in Locations that include group discussion, such as Chadder's Adventure Theater or Bible Adventures. (Plus, as kids carry out their crew roles, they'll all discover how important each crew member is!)

HolyWord HiNtS

Everyone can do the activities at HolyWord Studios! A physically challenged boy attended our field test, and he jumped right in and tried it all. Some activities were more challenging, but with the help of his crew members and a little flexibility, he was able to fully participate in every activity. What a wonderful reminder that God has special plans for all of us!

Learning Disabilities

Educators estimate that up to 20 percent of today's children have some type of learning disability. That means that in a program of one hundred children, up to twenty kids could be battling with dyslexia, attention-deficit/hyperactivity disorder, or other learning disabilities. Kids with learning disabilities aren't lazy or dumb—they just learn differently than other children do.

HolyWord Studios works for children with learning disabilities! Here's why:

- **It doesn't rely heavily on reading skills.** Children who enjoy reading can volunteer to be Readers for their Film Crews. Children who have trouble reading can choose other equally important jobs.
- **It allows kids processing time.** Because each Film Crew has a Film Crew Leader, Location Leaders don't have to single out kids who need special help. Crew lead-

ers can help the kids in their Film Crews work at their own pace. And Location Leaders are free to go around and check in with children as they complete their activities.

• **It doesn't require children to think sequentially.** Fifty percent of all students are frustrated by sequential-type assignments. At HolyWord Studios, children don't have to master a new set of information each day. Instead, they learn one basic Point that's reinforced in different ways for different kinds of learners.

If you know or suspect that kids with learning disabilities will be attending your program, let your teachers know. Encourage them to help these children by

• giving instructions one at a time,

• using the positive-language suggestions in the "What's a Film Crew Leader?" handout (p. 118),

• ignoring harmless annoying behaviors, and

• praising children sincerely and often.

For more information on attention-deficit/hyperactivity disorder (ADHD), use the address below to contact Children and Adults with Attention Deficit Disorders.

Children and Adults with Attention Deficit Disorders
8181 Professional Place, Suite 201
Landover, MD 20785

Welcoming Newcomers

Summer is a busy time for families. Some kids may come to HolyWord Studios all five days; some may come for two or three days and then drop out; others may join your HolyWord Studios program midcourse. Use the following ideas to welcome newcomers to your adventure.

• **Start with small Film Crews.** When you assign kids to Film Crews, limit some crews to three or four kids instead of five. If new kids join your program, you can assign them to Film Crews in which you've left openings. Even if you don't have many visitors, kids in smaller crews will love the additional attention they'll get from their Film Crew Leaders. If you want to encourage visitors to attend, challenge kids to fill their crews by inviting their friends!

• **Have kids introduce new Film Crew members.** Instead of escorting a visitor to a Film Crew yourself, invite one of the crew members to do it. Recruit an outgoing member of the visitor's assigned crew (a Cheerleader may be a good candidate for this job), and then introduce the visitor to the other child one on one. Help the child describe the Film Crew, including the crew name, the crew jobs, and the daily schedule. Then send the pair of children back to meet the rest of the crew.

• **Cheer for visitors each day during Sing & Play Soundtrack.** Have the Sing & Play Soundtrack Leader invite Film Crews to stand if they have new members. Have Cheerleaders introduce their new crew members; then have the Sing & Play Soundtrack Leader lead everyone in shouting, "Welcome!"

Responsibility: Let 'Em Have It!

At HolyWord Studios, Location Leaders provide fun, hands-on, Bible-learning activities. Film Crew Leaders shepherd and guide their Film Crews. But kids take responsibility for their own learning.

Even the most well-intentioned Location Leaders and Film Crew Leaders may be uncomfortable giving kids this much responsibility. After all, they're the leaders; they've prepared the material, and they know what kids should learn. Movie Munchies Leaders may insist that it's easier to prepare snacks ahead of time instead of counting on kids to complete the work. Film Crew Leaders may be tempted to complete Prop Shop Crafts projects for kids instead of helping them complete their own.

Every activity at your HolyWord Studios program has been field-tested, revised, retested, and revised again. So you can have confidence that kids will be able to follow directions and complete the activities successfully within the allotted times. Instead of doing kids' work for them, leaders should encourage Film Crew members to help kids star in God's story by helping each other complete activities.

By the end of the week, you'll hear reports of kids leading their own discussions, helping each other complete projects, and cheering each other on. Trust the Lord, and trust your kids—and watch God's love surround your program!

It's a Wrap!
Closing Program and Follow-Up Ideas

Helping Children Follow Jesus

At HolyWord Studios, children don't just hear about God's love—they see it, touch it, sing it, taste it, and put it into action. As they travel from Location to Location, they discover that the Bible is like a script for our lives. Most importantly, children learn that God sent his Son, Jesus, to die for our sins because he loves us.

You'll notice that there's no "set" time for children to make a faith commitment. We feel that HolyWord Studios helps children build relationships—with other children, adults, and with Jesus. And since each child is at a different point in his or her relationship with Jesus, programming a time for commitment may be confusing to some children. However, if it's part of your church tradition to include a time for children to make a faith decision, feel free to add it in during the Show Time on Day 4.

Some children may want to know more about making Jesus part of their lives. If you sense that a child might like to know more about what it means to follow Jesus, give this simple explanation:

God loves us so much that he sent his Son, Jesus, to die on the cross for us. Jesus died and rose again so we could be forgiven for all the wrong things we do. Jesus wants to be our forever friend. If we ask him to, he'll take away the wrong things we've done and fill our lives with his love. As our forever friend, Jesus will always be with us and will help us make the right choices. And if we believe in Jesus, someday we'll live with him forever in heaven.

You may want to lead the child in a simple prayer inviting Jesus to be his or her forever friend. You may also want to share one or more of the following Scripture passages with the child. Encourage the child to read the Scripture passages with you from his or her own Bible.

- John 3:16
- Romans 5:8-11
- Romans 6:23
- Ephesians 2:5-8

Be sure to share the news of the child's spiritual development with his or her parent(s).

Take Five, Everyone!

Thanks for joining us at Group's HolyWord Studios! Now that you've "wrapped" your studio production, you can sit back, take five, and congratulate yourself and your cast on a fine performance. Then thank God for his blessings on your program. In this section, you'll find ideas that will help you to wrap up your program and follow up with children and their families. You'll also find helpful evaluation forms you can use to get specific feedback from Location Leaders and Film Crew Leaders.

Closing Program: The Grand Finale

If you want an easy way to give parents and church members a glimpse of your HolyWord Studios fun, invite them to attend Show Time. This fun-filled, Bible-learning time is already built in to your HolyWord Studios program each day. Explain that parents can join the fun by arriving just twenty minutes early when they come to pick up their children. They'll see children singing Sing & Play Soundtrack songs, telling what they did on location, and actively reviewing the daily Bible story. Parents will really catch the HolyWord Studios spirit as children celebrate God's love with a grand celebration on Day 5.

If you want to have a separate closing program, follow the steps below to set up a Location "open house." Set up your open house in the evening or even on Sunday morning. Parents and kids will love it!

1. Have Location Leaders set up the following activities in their respective Location areas. If you purchased additional *Sing & Play Soundtrack* audiocassettes, encourage Location Leaders to play the HolyWord Studios songs while people are visiting their areas.

Sing & Play Soundtrack—Have the Sing & Play Soundtrack Leader teach words and motions to all thirteen songs (or as many as time allows).

Preschool Bible Playhouse—Have the Preschool Bible Playhouse Director set up five or six Location Stations children can visit with their parents. Choose from the activities suggested below, or let the Preschool Director suggest kids' favorites!

- Love Loom
- Basket of Babies
- Singin' in the Rain
- Roll Back the Sea

Prop Shop Crafts—Have the Prop Shop Crafts Leader display his or her sample Prop Shop Crafts projects (or have kids display the crafts they made—if they're willing to part with them for a little while). Ask the crafts leader to explain the stories of Ken Ken, Sanja, and Jelani on the Operation Kid-to-Kid posters. Have the crafts leader encourage kids to show their parents the contents of a sample Care Kit.

Now Playing Games—Have the Games Leader lead families in the water balloon game kids played on Day 1 or River Run (also from Day 1). Families will also enjoy Under Attack, Socks on Your Head, or the All-Star Olympics.

Movie Munchies—Have the Movie Munchies Leader set out supplies for making Bugs and Blood. Display a sample snack, and let children and parents make their own tasty treats.

Chadder's Adventure Theater—Have the Chadder's Adventure Theater Leader play the *Chadder's HolyWord Adventure* video. Set out paper, markers, and pencils, and let families "storyboard" possible further adventures for Chadder, Carmine, and Hoppy. Or kids can use the extra Bible story stickers (on their HolyWord Studios sticker sheets) to mark where the Bible stories are in their Bibles.

Blockbuster Bible Adventures—Have the Blockbuster Bible Adventures Leader set up the Passover door posts. Allow families to paint the doorways and pray for family members. Or invite Pharaoh to make a "guest appearance" and walk families through all of the plagues.

Show Time—Have the Show Time Leader lead people in the show from Day 3. Select audience members to be the Israelites, while everyone else acts as the wild, wavy Red Sea! (This is a great visual show that family members of all ages will delight in!)

2. Begin by having everyone gather in the sanctuary or the fellowship hall for a brief introduction and a Sing & Play Soundtrack time. Have your Sing & Play Soundtrack Leader teach everyone "God's Story." This is a great time to distribute HolyWord Studios completion certificates. Simply photocopy the certificates on pages 180 and 181 (or purchase the "And the Winner Is..." certificates); fill in children's, Film Crew Leaders', or Location Leaders' names; then sign and date each certificate.

3. Designate a thirty- to forty-five-minute time frame in which families can visit the Locations. At the end of the designated time, use a hand clapper to call everyone back to your original meeting area for Show Time.

4. Thank everyone for coming, and encourage them to join you in planning and preparing for next year's program.

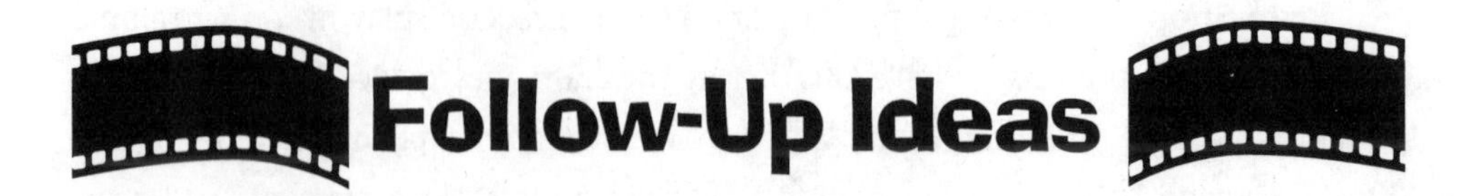

Follow-Up Ideas

Your HolyWord Studios has ended. But helping kids know and love God never ends. You still have lots of time to share the good news about Jesus with the kids in your church and community. The outreach efforts you make will help you share God's love with your HolyWord Studios participants and their families. Use the ideas below to design a follow-up plan that fits your church's needs.

- **Send HolyWord Studios follow-up postcards.** Kids love getting mail, so here's a sure-fire way to get kids back for Sunday school—a personal invitation from HolyWord Studios. These colorful postcards help you make a long-term impact on kids by involving them in your regular Sunday school program. *Order these postcards from Group Publishing or your local Christian bookstore.*
- **Give away HolyWord Studios photos.** Deliver framed photos to families of children who don't regularly attend your church. Kids will treasure these colorful, fun mementos—and you'll have an opportunity to invite the family to visit your church. *Order HolyWord Studios photo frames from Group Publishing or your local Christian bookstore.*
- **Invite Chadder Chipmunk to visit a children's ministry event.** Schedule a return engagement of *Chadder's HolyWord Adventure* during another children's ministry event. Children who visited your church during HolyWord Studios will want to come back and revisit their furry friend. Add a live appearance from a Chadder plush puppet, and you'll be sure to fill every chair! *Order Chadder plush puppets and* Chadder's HolyWord Adventure *videocassettes from Group Publishing or your local Christian bookstore.*
- **Sponsor a parents day.** Build relationships with children's parents by having a parents day during HolyWord Studios. Encourage children to invite their parents or older siblings to join them. Provide adult and youth Bible studies or have family members visit the Locations with their children's Film Crews. Also require parents to come inside to pick up their children so you can make contact with them.
- **Hold a HolyWord Studios memory night.** Invite all the HolyWord Studios participants to a get-together every month or every quarter. Make each memory night a fun event that fits the HolyWord Studios theme. This is an excellent time to host the HolyWord Academy Awards. Create silly awards (or have kids create a few) that everyone

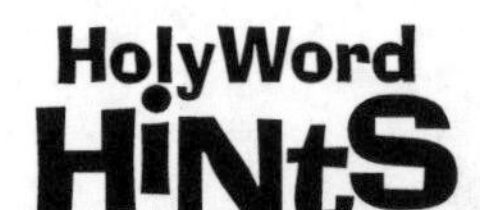

Now that Chadder has gone back to explore Bible times, you can easily "send" him back again for other children's ministry events. Are you covering the Creation story? Maybe Chadder's time machine can pop in and add to your story. Jonah and the big fish? Perhaps Chadder can check it out and report back to you! Use your imagination...you can bet the kids in your classes will!

can enjoy, and that will remind kids and adults of the fun they had at HolyWord Studios.

• **Thank your cast members for all their hard work.** Your praise and appreciation will speak volumes to your volunteers...and can be integral in their decision to volunteer next year. So go the extra mile to show them how much you appreciate all they've done. A card with a personal, heartfelt message is always a good idea. Balloons, flowers, or baked goodies are even better. You might consider filling popcorn bags with movie treats and even a gift certificate to a video rental store or local movie theater. Include a package of microwavable popcorn, along with a note that says, "Your energy kept us all popping this week." A box of Good & Plenty candies could accompany the note: "Your love for children was good and plenty at VBS!" Or drop in a box of Junior Mints with the note, "Your smile was so refreshing. Thanks for all you did for our HolyWord Studios Production."

• **Sign up a cast for next year's production.** It's never too early to start recruiting, and your cast and crew will be excited about the week they've just finished at HolyWord Studios. There's no better time to collect the "autographs" of volunteers who might be interested in volunteering for next year's VBS program. Photocopy the "Encore! A Repeat Performance!" handout on page 183 and post it around your facility. You may be surprised at the jump-start you'll get on next year's recruitment!

And The Winner Is...
Thanks for Your Important Role in
Helping Kids Star in God's Story!
You've been an all-star ______ Leader.
HolyWord Studios Director
Date

And The Winner Is...
Thanks for starring in God's amazing story at
HolyWord Studios VBS™
HolyWord Studios Director
Date

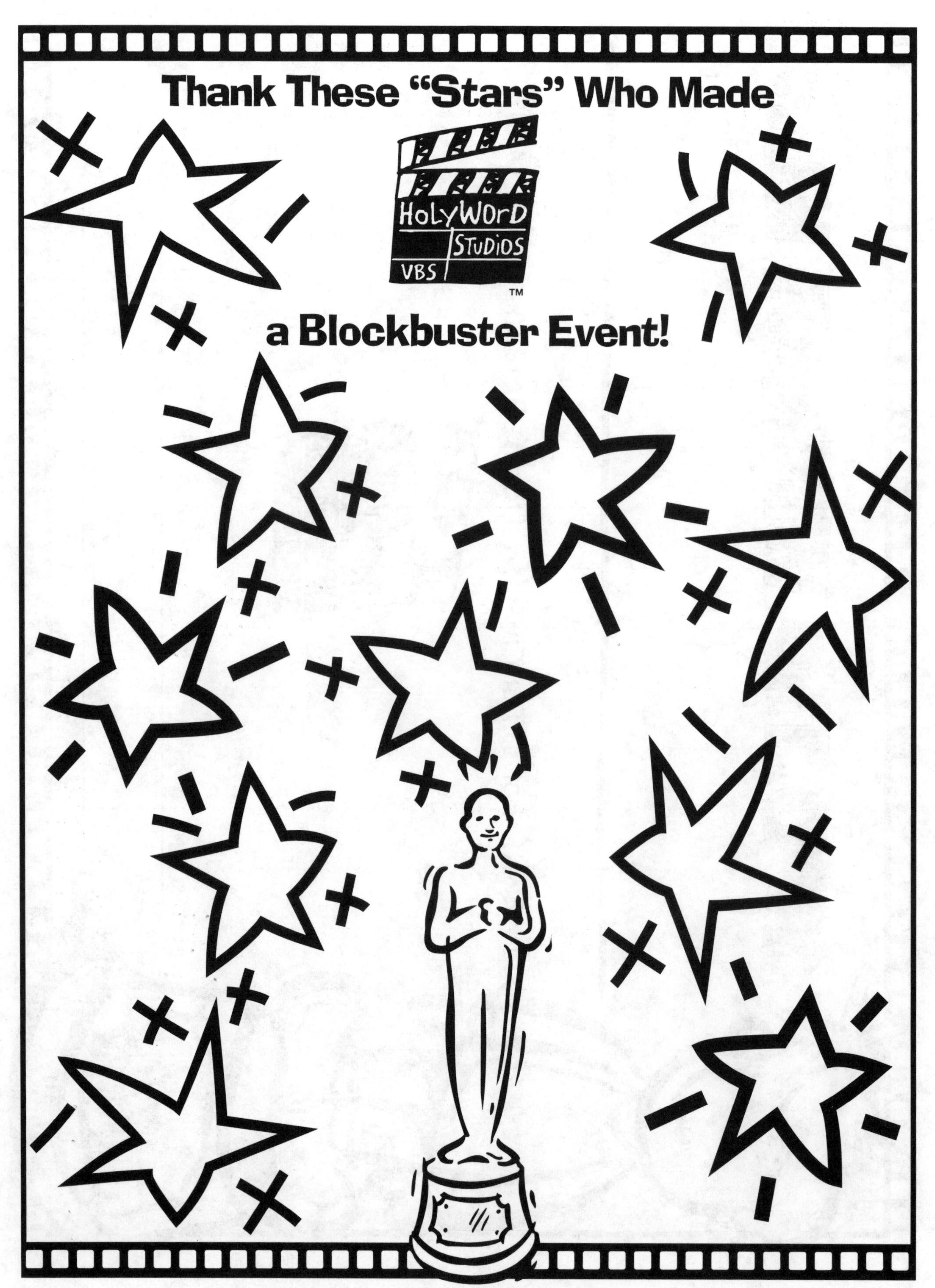
Thank These "Stars" Who Made
HolyWord
Studios
VBS
™
a Blockbuster Event!

Encore!

A Repeat Performance!

Your role in this year's HolyWord Studios production was a smash hit! We'd love to book you for a repeat performance at next year's VBS. If you're interested, just autograph below. We'll hang on to your name and information and let you know what casting opportunities are available next year.

Name	Phone	At next year's VBS, I would be interested in...

Evaluating Your HolyWord Studios Program

HolyWord HiNtS

You can customize the evaluation forms by adding additional questions in the "Other comments about our HolyWord Studios program" section. For example, you may want to ask about facilities or about the dates and times of your VBS. This is also a good time to recruit volunteers for next year's VBS. Location Leaders and Film Crew Leaders will have had so much fun that they'll want to sign on again!

After HolyWord Studios, you'll want to check in with your Location Leaders, Film Crew Leaders, and other staff members to see how things went.

Photocopy the "Location Leader VBS Evaluation" (p. 185) and the "Film Crew Leader VBS Evaluation" (p. 186), and distribute the photocopies to your staff. To help your evaluation process go smoothly, you may want to ask staff members to return their evaluations within two weeks of HolyWord Studios. After two weeks, specific details will still be fresh in staff members' minds, and they'll have a good perspective on their overall experiences.

After you've collected Location Leader and Film Crew Leader evaluation forms, please take a few moments to fill out the "HolyWord Studios Evaluation" on pages 187-188. Be sure to summarize the comments you received from Location Leaders and Film Crew Leaders. Keep a copy of your completed evaluation for your records; then return the original to Group's VBS Coordinator. Your detailed feedback will help us meet your needs as we plan an all-new program for next year.

Thanks for choosing Group's HolyWord Studios!

Location Leader VBS Evaluation

Thanks for joining us at HolyWord Studios! Please complete this evaluation form to help us plan for next year's VBS.

1. I led the ____ Location.

2. I spent ______________ minutes preparing materials for each day.

3. Were the instructions in your Location leader manual clear and easy to follow? Explain.

4. What did you like best about your Location? What did kids like best?

5. What would you like to change about your Location?

Other comments about our HolyWord Studios program:

Film Crew Leader VBS Evaluation

Thanks for joining us at HolyWord Studios! Please complete this evaluation form to help us plan for next year's VBS.

1. What was the best thing about working with your Film Crew?

2. What was the hardest thing?

3. Did the "For Film Crew Leaders Only" handouts help you as you worked with kids? Explain.

4. What other training helps or resources would have helped you in your Film Crew Leader role?

HolyWord Studios Evaluation

We appreciate your joining us for unforgettable, fun Bible learning...and we look forward to introducing you to an all-new VBS next year!

Will you help us make next year's VBS even better? Take a few moments at the end of your program to fill out this survey. Drop it in the mail, and let us know what you think!

Thank you!

Jody Brolsma

Jody Brolsma
HolyWord Studios Coordinator

1. What was the number one reason you chose Group's HolyWord Studios?

FOLD FOLD

2. Tell us how you learned about Group's HolyWord Studios.

❍ Bookstore ❍ Mailing ❍ Advertisement ❍ Other (please specify)

3. Where did you purchase your VBS items?

❍ Bookstore ❍ Direct from Group

Why?

4. In what month do you choose your upcoming VBS program?
In what month do you order materials?

5. Tell us how you liked the HolyWord Studios program.

❍ I loved it! I can't wait to see next year's! ❍ It was OK—it met my VBS needs.
❍ It didn't work at all for my church.

What, if anything, would you like us to change or improve?

6. Tell us what was most difficult for you in putting together HolyWord Studios?

FOLD FOLD

What could we do to make your job easier?

7. Tell us what you liked most about the HolyWord Studios Director Manual.

What would you change about the HolyWord Studios Director Manual?

8. Tell us about the music at your VBS.

Check which of the following you used in your Sing & Play sessions?

❍ *Sing & Play Soundtrack* audiocassette
❍ *Sing & Play Soundtrack Music Video*
❍ *Sing & Play Soundtrack Music & Clip Art CD*
❍ *Sing & Play Transparencies*
❍ piano or guitar accompaniment

Did you use the clip art on the CD?

Would you use lyrics on PowerPoint if they were made available?

9. Tell us how you set up your VBS

❍ five consecutive days ❍ five consecutive evenings ❍ a weekend program

❍ as a midweek program, spanning several weeks ❍ other (explain)

What did you have to adapt most?

10. Tell us about Operation Kid-to-Kid™.

How many Care Kits did your church prepare?

Where did you send the Care Kits?

What did you like about the mission project?

11. Did you ever check out our VBS Web site (grouppublishing.com and/or ok2k.org)? If so, do you have any suggestions for things we could add or improve?

12. We're always looking for fun and innovative themes for our VBS programs. What new ideas would your kids like to see in the future?

FOLD FOLD

13. Would you recommend Group's VBS to a friend?

❍ Yes, because...

❍ No, because...

14. If you've seen a life changed as a result of your VBS, please share the story.

If you said something nice about Group's VBS, may we quote you? ❍ Yes

Please fold on dotted lines with the below flap facing outside and tape closed. Thank you.

NAME

ADDRESS

CITY STATE ZIP

NO POSTAGE NECESSARY IF MAILED IN THE UNITED STATES

BUSINESS REPLY MAIL

FIRST-CLASS MAIL PERMIT NO 16 LOVELAND CO

POSTAGE WILL BE PAID BY ADDRESSEE

VBS COORDINATOR
P.O. BOX 481
LOVELAND, CO 80539-9985

Index